What Readers Are Saying
'The Obstacle Course' by N

D1129196

"This quick-paced story entertains, enlightens and is filled with pearls of wisdom that will inspire positive change in a loved one's life. So, do your loved ones a favor, buy them a copy!"

Ken D. Foster
Best-Selling Author, *Ask and You Will Succeed*,
and CEO, Shared Vision Network
http://www.Ask-Succeed.com

~ ~ ~ ~ ~ ~ ~ ~ ~

"I have studied and published self-help information for many years, and rarely do I see something as unique and fresh as *The Obstacle Course*.

Its story format is fun and entertaining to read, while making it easier to understand and remember the lessons... And these lessons are some of the most important things to know in life, things which aren't typically learned in school.

I believe anyone can take a course from 'Dr. Acton', benefit from this book, and enjoy the story at the same time."

Steve Moore
Editor/Webmaster, Personal-Development.Com
http://www.Personal-Development.com

~ ~ ~ ~ ~ ~ ~ ~ ~

"*The Obstacle Course* is one of those books that you will find yourself reading over and over again. And each time you read it, you'll come away better than you were before. You'll have a better perspective on life, your place in it, and the way you look at it. Prepare to be changed forever after reading this amazing work."

Andy O'Bryan
Founder, Principal Visions, LLC
http://www.IncentiveToolkit.com

~ ~ ~ ~ ~ ~ ~ ~ ~

"*The Obstacle Course* is in the same genre as *Who Moved My Cheese?*, but has its own unique labyrinth of stories that not only entertain, but move and challenge the reader to think about larger issues.

The story has special applications to those in academia and especially those in business. *The Obstacle Course* touches the realm of spirituality without being overtly religious or sectarian. To that extent, it is a book for everyone.

Rather than being another 'how-to' book, *The Obstacle Course* is lightly seasoned with humor that makes for an enjoyable read that touches the soul as well as the mind."

Kenneth M. Lankin, M.D.
Founder, Dr. Lankin's Specialty Foods, LLC
http://www.AwesomeAlmonds.com

~ ~ ~ ~ ~ ~ ~ ~ ~

"I'm a firm believer that – right along with teaching math, reading, and history – our schools and universities should be teaching the ideas that are shared in this novel. Everyone can benefit from the lessons that Dr. Acton teaches in *The Obstacle Course*.

Neal R. Voron has a winner in this book… and, in this case, you'll receive the rewards in your life from applying the principles shared."

Josh Hinds
CEO, GetMotivation.com
Publisher, "Let's Talk Motivation!" newsletter
http://www.GetMotivation.com

~ ~ ~ ~ ~ ~ ~ ~ ~

"*The Obstacle Course* is a clever, cerebral, thought-provoking adventure in pedagogy. Dr. Ernest Acton is a professor, philosopher and motivator, and Neal R. Voron is a storyteller par excellence who introduces us to the teacher we all wish we had."

Donald R. Stoltz, D.O.
Physician, Children's Book Author, and
Author of Books About Norman Rockwell
http://www.DrDonaldStoltz.com

~ ~ ~ ~ ~ ~ ~ ~ ~

"*The Obstacle Course* is just that – a course about obstacles and how they affect our futures. Although this short book is written in a fictional form, it is actually a guide to self-realization that carries numerous truths – many which we may have always known, but lately have put aside in the pace of the day, and many that may be new to our thinking.

The sum total of **The Obstacle Course** reminds us that the single most important obstacle in life is ourselves.

This is a book for students – both formal learners and life-long learners. As a former teacher, I see **The Obstacle Course** as a wonderful supplement to any classroom experience. It encourages students to take charge of their goals and of their own education.

Each chapter is a springboard for a spirited discussion session. There are exercises that can be duplicated in the classroom and even a short page of review questions at the end.

If you are looking for something to inspire and lighten your day, **The Obstacle Course** will meet the challenge. If you are a teacher, you owe it to yourself to investigate this tool."

Janna McGlasson
Former Drama Teacher
Co-Host, Cheap Thrills Bookstore
http://members.aol.com/jannakaren/

~ ~ ~ ~ ~ ~ ~ ~ ~

"A fast, fun, mind-expanding good read."

Joe Vitale
Best-Selling Author, "Spiritual Marketing",
"The Greatest Money-Making Secret In History!",
"Hypnotic Writing", and Other Books
http://www.MrFire.com

~ ~ ~ ~ ~ ~ ~ ~ ~

"*The Obstacle Course*, written by Neal R. Voron, is a literary prescription. I recommend it for all ages. It is a story filled with mental calisthenics... Doctor Acton teaches his students and you, the reader, how to be aware and to take positive action when faced with an unexpected or an expected obstacle.

Refreshing, stimulating, offering you a challenge to ignite the power of positive thought... Mr. Voron has a whimsical way of storytelling, opening your mind to truth, as Plato and Aristotle did... Clarity versus veiled uncertainty.

Every school and library should have this humanitarian self-help book as a staple."

Joseph F.M. Pokorny
Songwriter, Musician, Composer
Co-Founder with Neal R. Voron of RyKy Records (tm)
http://www.RyKyRecords.com

Note: Mr. Pokorny was so inspired by the story that he has created *The Obstacle Course Musical!*

~ ~ ~ ~ ~ ~ ~ ~ ~

"Read this book! Fast-paced, entertaining and most importantly, it'll get "under your skin" and transform your life. Great reading. Great fun. The principles are powerful, practical and timeless. Once again – buy and read this book!"

Philip E. Humbert, Ph.D.
Author, Keynote Speaker and Personal Success Strategist
http://www.PhilipHumbert.com

~ ~ ~ ~ ~ ~ ~ ~ ~

"*The Obstacle Course* is written as a novel, but to me, as a person who has been in therapy for clinical depression, it is more of a self-help/inspirational book.

The seemingly simple teaching method Dr. Acton uses enables his students to overcome obstacles they hadn't even thought of as being obstacles. By doing this and by using his unique teaching methods, Dr. Acton is able to instill in his students confidence and self-awareness that obstacles and the path to overcome them are truly possible. He also instills in his students a deep feeling of self-worth and compassion that is truly inspiring.

I highly recommend this book to anyone, young or old, simply because it makes you feel good – and that is a rare commodity in the times we live in."

Marci Pearl

~ ~ ~ ~ ~ ~ ~ ~ ~

'Prepare to be changed forever after reading this amazing work.' – Andy O'Bryan

Neal R. Voron

The
OBSTACLE
COURSE

… A Self-Help/Inspirational Novel

authorHOUSE™

1663 LIBERTY DRIVE, SUITE 200
BLOOMINGTON, INDIANA 47403
(800) 839-8640
WWW.AUTHORHOUSE.COM

© 2005 Neal R. Voron. All Rights Reserved.

No part of this book may be reproduced, stored in a retrieval system, or transmitted by any means without the written permission of the author.

First published by AuthorHouse 01/26/05

ISBN: 1-4184-6603-4 (e-book)
ISBN: 1-4184-4739-0 (softcover)

Printed in the United States of America
Bloomington, Indiana

This book is printed on acid-free paper.

For information about joining the **"Dr. Acton Fan Club"**,
visit: **http://www.TheObstacleCourse.com**

... *Dedication* ...

This book is dedicated to entertaining you and to "making a difference" in your life.

It is my hope that this story helps to open your mind to life's possibilities, enabling you to gain insight into your own answers to those things that are most important to you.

I wish you great success in the "obstacle course" of life!

Neal R. Voron
nvoron@TheObstacleCourse.com

... *Acknowledgements* ...

The author gratefully acknowledges the influence of both professional and "life" teachers who have encouraged the pursuit of knowledge, questioning, brainstorming, play, creativeness, independent thinking, debate, and application of knowledge.

Special thanks to my family and friends – especially to my wife, **Barbarann**, to my parents, **Babs** and **Vic Voron**, to my twin brother, **Dave Voron**, and to my sisters, **Sharyn Voron-Bultena** and **Ellyn Glass** – who have encouraged me and supported my endeavors over the years to make a positive impact upon society.

Thanks, too, to **Sharol Brunner** and the *Eggnoggin Heads* team and to **Joseph F.M. Pokorny** for stoking my passion to bring Dr. Acton and his important messages to greater audiences to both entertain and enlighten.

Your thoughts and actions mean so much!

... Foreword ...

By **Sharol Brunner**, B.A., Education
Teacher, Elementary Education

The Obstacle Course is the "classroom" experience of a lifetime. Don't put this book down until you have read it, or you will miss a great opportunity to be educated in a most unusual way. Whether you are ten years old, or 100 years old, this book will give you simple insight into some of life's toughest and greatest lessons.

The Obstacle Course is fun and enjoyable reading, filled with suspense and anticipation. Author Neal R. Voron has captured a style and quality that will entice even the youngest of readers to take this "advanced course" and reap its benefits.

All you need is the desire to learn, and this book will give you the tools to help you achieve your own personal goals. Do not expect immediate answers; expect the unexpected and some interesting insights. If you want to learn in a more traditional and serious manner, look elsewhere. *The Obstacle Course* is for you if you're willing to enjoy yourself while you are being taught.

This book must be read in order, from beginning to end, to experience the fullness of its message. After reading it the first time, you will want to join this classroom setting again and again in order to continue your education and gain insight. The page-turning quality and the writing style will keep you coming back for more.

I found **The Obstacle Course** on the Internet, quite by chance, before its print publication when it was only available in an electronic format. The first 5 chapters of the story were offered for free reading, and I shared them with several of my fourth grade students. They immediately wanted to read more, and I contacted the author, Neal R. Voron, directly to obtain some copies. My students' response to the story was highly favorable. Since then, all of our lives have taken on new and enlightened perspectives to apply in our everyday situations.

In the story, Dr. Acton is the professor the students are all waiting for – someone to challenge them and to make learning interesting.

The characters in the novel are easily recognizable, having many of the preconceived notions and mindsets which so often block our ability to learn...

When my students were presented with a challenging problem to solve, they quickly began to draw upon their own, very limited past experiences. It was my challenge as their teacher and coach to open their hearts and minds to new ways of looking at very familiar situations. Rather than direct them to the answers, my goal was to challenge them to seek and find their own new and creative answers.

Eager and enthusiastic learners, my students absorb most academic information readily. Born with strong senses' of justice, and right and wrong, social and philosophical lessons are often overlooked with these children. Yet these very lessons are also important to teach in order to help them see that there is more than one way (their way) to look at any given situation.

By reading this book, my students have learned that change can be good, to be prepared for the unexpected, to take on challenges with curiosity and anticipation, and to expect to fail sometimes but not to give up on their goals. What great lessons!

This book has an approach and creative style of teaching that can, and should, be used more often in our classrooms. It could be used effectively as a teaching tool in many settings, from school counseling offices, team building sessions, to larger classroom environments.

Take this book home or to your place of work, read it aloud to your family or friends, or keep it to yourself... but guaranteed when you reach the last page, you will have completed a course of life lessons that you will take out into your life!

Chapter 1

There was an excitement in the air unlike any phenomenon I had ever experienced before. The anticipation of the arriving crowd of anxious students was that something wonderful was about to happen... and it was going to happen any minute now... to us, to all of us!

In small groups – one, two, three students at a time – we filtered through the doorway. The gathering class increasingly became transformed into a frenetic group of fidgeting and high-pitched, fast-speaking, but enthusiastic, conversationalists. The room was so abuzz with such supercharged energy that goosebumps appeared on my arms and I sat away from the window lest I get struck by lightning.

We were all eager to begin what was rumored by other students to be "the most worthwhile course you'll ever take."

Naturally, we wanted to know why the course was so terrific, but the standard reply always was, "you'll have to find out for yourself!" The words were always spoken with great enthusiasm – as from souls who had found a new self-confidence, a sense of purpose – and they always sounded sincere in their encouragement to take the course, as if they wanted to bestow upon us a secret gift. When college students speak with that much enthusiasm about a class, either they're playing a cruel prank or they're letting you in on something special. I decided to take a chance and find out for myself.

So, there we were... a full house – 40 desk chairs, 40 students – 20 men, 20 women – awaiting "The Obstacle Course", taught by Dr. Ernest T. Acton, known to the fortunate few as a truly remarkable "teacher" in the fullest sense of the word.

And then there was a roar of thunder outside, and you could hear a torrent of rain driving hard down from the sky, riveting the outer world with drops of polluted water as the horizon flickered with momentary illumination. As if on cue, the atmospheric distractions coincided with the entry of Dr. Acton into the room.

Chapter 2

What a shock! Not having met Dr. Acton before, I had no idea of what to expect in terms of his appearance, his manners, his methods... Somehow, I had visualized him as being in his mid-40's, well toned, perhaps 6'3", weighing 200 pounds, with a full head of dark, shining, wavy hair, and a glowing complexion.

Galloping into the room with a quick, direct stride was a man who looked to be nearing 70, about 5'5", 130 pounds, with a huge, shining bald spot trimmed with white hair, and a complexion that clearly had seen many days. Dr. Acton looked remarkably like my paternal grandfather, but he seemed to have two conspicuous attributes that belied any frailties he may have possessed: his hazel eyes radiated with life, and his cheeks formed a ready, easy smile that made him seem personable.

Placing his tattered and worn burgundy leather portfolio atop his desk, he leaned his side against the desk so as to be half-sitting.

"Good evening!" he greeted the class with seemingly sincere enthusiasm. "My name is Dr. Ernest T. Acton, and I am so glad that so many of you made a decision to fit this evening course into your busy schedules. It is a wise move for those of you who are serious about accomplishing things that are important to you in your life."

"'The Obstacle Course' is a class about dealing with life's happenings and the things you would like to happen," Dr. Acton continued. "If you want this course to be helpful to you, open your mind to it. I will work hard to help you learn."

"Okay, class dismissed!" he said, his voice raising with excitement. "See you next week!" he said, as he grabbed his portfolio and then quickly walked out of the room.

We were all stunned. We could not believe what had just happened: he basically just came in, said 'hello', and left! A few guys in the class quickly ran into the hallway, hoping to corner Dr. Acton and find out why he did that. Most of us just sat there in the room, dumbfounded. We waited a few minutes until our classmates returned with their report: "We couldn't find him! He disappeared!"

"Why did he leave?" we wondered. "Were we victims of somebody's joke?" More than a few students weren't too amused with the evening's events. I must say, I, too, was disappointed.

Chapter 3

When the class met again, several faces were missing. Before Dr. Acton arrived, there were a number of discussions about why he may have left so abruptly the previous week. The consensus opinion was that he probably prefers a brief introductory first meeting. But, we were curious, why hadn't he at least handed out a course syllabus and list of reading materials? We were determined to find out.

Dr. Acton galloped in promptly at 7 p.m. just as he had for the first meeting.

"Good Evening!" he cheerfully greeted his audience, his smile brimming widely while he tossed his portfolio onto the desk.

The smile was not returned.

"Oh, I see," he said, surveying the dour faces and seven empty desk chairs. "Even though some of your classmates were able to overcome any obstacles last week that may have prevented them from taking this evening class, they apparently were unable to overcome the obstacles they faced this week. That's too bad."

John, one of the students who had tried, unsuccessfully, to catch up with Dr. Acton last week, then jumped up from his seat. "Dr. Acton, why did you leave so abruptly last week? We were all excited about getting started with our classwork! You didn't even give us a course syllabus or a reading list!"

"Young man," the old man replied, "I left because the lesson was over. This class is about dealing with life's happenings and the things you would like to happen. I said that if you want this course to be helpful to you, you must open your mind to it. If you are to learn, you must think. Prior to last week, you – all of you – had set a goal to take this course. Last week, you embarked on a path toward your goal and overcame any obstacles – such as the time of the meeting – that may have gotten in the way. That was good! But it was also fairly easy…"

"Easy?" I asked aloud, not realizing Dr. Acton had heard me.

"Yes, my friend. I think perhaps having to adjust one's schedule to accommodate participating in an activity for which you have high interest is not too difficult an obstacle for most people," he replied. "The anticipation and excitement level shown by the class last week when I entered the room was extraordinarily high. It's much more difficult to overcome obstacles when the enthusiasm for achieving your goal has dimmed somewhat or when a tougher obstacle gets in the way. My quick departure last week seems to have drawn a few of your classmates off the path."

"Why do you think that happened?" John interjected, still a bit miffed.

"Let me ask you," Dr. Acton retorted. "Why do you think that happened?"

"Well, because they probably didn't think it would be worth their time to continue in class. Maybe they thought they would be throwing their money away. Or perhaps they thought you were too strange to learn anything worthwhile from, considering the way you left so suddenly," John replied.

I cringed upon hearing that! John was being awfully bold!

"You may be right, young man," Dr. Acton said, "Your fellow classmates may have left the class for any or all of those reasons or for some other reason. But the reasons you suggest represent an obstacle that stops many people from ever accomplishing things they originally set out to do. That obstacle is 'uncertainty'."

"Class, the differences between you who are attending class today and your classmates who decided not to attend are clear: they allowed obstacles to block their path to learning the material for this class; you did not allow obstacles to block your path, and you are learning new lessons here today."

"Now, son," Dr. Acton continued, addressing John, "your questions regarding a syllabus and reading list seem to confirm my assessment of the class' unreadiness to learn last week..."

"Unreadiness to learn?" I heard myself question.

Dr. Acton had heard me, too.

"Yes," he turned towards me, "unreadiness." He grabbed the leather portfolio from his desk. "Look," he said, unzipping the portfolio to show the entire class that it was empty, "there's no syllabus, no reading list!"

We were astounded. "Why?" we asked collectively. "How will we learn?" one student asked. "How will we get graded?" asked another.

Dr. Acton replied, "Think about it."

The old man paused for a moment, smiled, enthusiastically said, "See you next week!", and walked quickly out the door.

Nobody chased after him. We had a few things to think about.

Chapter 4

Think about things, we did. But we had more questions than answers. In fact, we still didn't have much of a clue about what Dr. Acton and "The Obstacle Course" were all about.

Why didn't Dr. Acton give some structure to the class? If he was following a lesson plan, why didn't he let us know the schedule? What did he expect from us? And, yes, what about grades? When the course is over, how will we know how well we did?... And another thing... Why did the old man carry around an old, soft-leather briefcase that's empty? What was the purpose?

That question intrigued me because everything Dr. Acton said and did seemed so purposeful. Yet, his actions and his reactions seemed to occur so spontaneously! He possessed an extraordinary sense of control – so extraordinary that we wondered whether anything could rattle him.

I wasn't the only one so intrigued. In fact, word spread quickly among my classmates that someone devised a plan to "trick" the dear doctor. He was going to be in for a surprise, and everyone was anxious about what would happen. Not only did the 33 of us from last week show up for class, but so did two others who had attended the first week.

What was "the trick" going to be? I felt a pang of guilt as Dr. Acton galloped into the room promptly at 7 p.m.

"Good evening, everyone!" the unsuspecting leader said with a smile as he propped up his portfolio on the desk. "Good evening!" was the reply in unison.

"Is this a newfound enthusiasm, or have you all conjured up some answers to the questions you posed last week?" Dr. Acton asked.

John was first to reply. "Doctor, you threw our questions back at us again. How are we to find the answers?"

"Good question, son! How are we to find the answers? WE ASK!" the wise man said.

"But, we did ask..." John said.

Dr. Acton then interjected, "Sometimes you must ask, ask, and ask again to get the information you want. Give up, and what will you have?... NO ANSWER!!! You must know what you want to ask; you must know how to ask it; you must figure out who to ask it of – and sometimes you need only to ask it again of yourself because YOU have answers within you to questions that have not been asked!"

"So, now I ask again," John implored. "Why haven't we been given a course syllabus and a reading list, Dr. Acton?"

"My friend," he finally obliged, "the answer is simply because you don't need them for this course. You are here, in class. If you pay attention, if you open your mind, if you think about what is discussed, if you ask questions, if you seek the answers, if you understand the concepts, if you utilize those concepts in your everyday life, you will LEARN and you will continue to learn for as long as you practice these things."

He continued, gazing throughout the audience, "I want your minds focused on learning about obstacles and how to deal with them. You will learn by earnest, thoughtful action, not by locking your minds to some inflexible guideline that assumes authority simply because it has been committed to paper!"

Suddenly, the door to the room closed with a click. "Don't bother getting it," Acton instructed. "Let's not let anything interrupt this discussion."

There was a brief shuffling of bodies in their seats in the back of the room, and a quick glance back revealed some not-too-well-concealed smiles.

The teacher continued, "Regarding a reading list, YOU KNOW what you have to read to learn about things that you need to know and YOU KNOW what you have to read to learn about things that are important to you. If you don't know, you can find out by ASKING. Reading is your responsibility. All I will say is don't let lack of knowledge or lack of ability to acquire knowledge become an obstacle in your lives. It doesn't have to be. YOU can decide about that."

"Uh, Doctor, what about grades?" came a voice from the far end of the room.

The old man winced as if his most heartfelt prose had just been pierced by a sling of outrageous fortune.

He stared icily ahead, quickly and boldly moving his eyes from one to another of us, seemingly searching to connect with the inner vision deep beyond the surface of our brows. There was just a brief second of almost breathless anticipation, and then came a jarring SILENCE. Dr. Acton merely leaned against the desk, rested his chin upon his open palm, and stared at us.

After about a minute, he spoke, softly, addressing the questioner in form, but the class in posture. "What about grades? Why do you think I haven't mentioned grades?"

Everyone remained silent.

"If you focus on grades, your perceptions of this class may not be broad enough to include whole spheres of opportunities for your minds to grow. You may ruin the fun, shut down the creativity, get stuck on form, and never see the path to what is most important."

He continued, "Your participation in this class is most relevant to me; your grades are not. Those who journey on 'The Obstacle Course' always learn where they stand."

"If you are afraid about what grade you will receive, I give you two choices: leave the class now, and don't worry about it; or stay in the class, and do not worry about it! Do yourselves a favor – leave your worries at the door. Come to class – pay attention, think, learn, and use what you learn – and you will do well."

"…Now, let us get on with the course!" he said, clapping his hands with excitement. No one rushed toward the door.

Suddenly, it appeared something wonderful was about to happen: Dr. Acton was about to teach!

Chapter 5

The old man turned towards the blackboard and reached for a piece of chalk. For the first time, notebooks opened and caps lifted off from many pens.

He wrote just one word, L-E-A-R-N. "Learn".

"Please put your notebooks away," the teacher implored. "You will not need them. The core of learning is listening, you hear? You must listen to what is being taught! When we couple listening with thinking about what is said, we begin to gain some understanding based upon this new information and our previous knowledge and experiences. Once we have some understanding of a topic, we can use that information to help understand other topics."

"In this course, L-E-A-R-N, 'Learn,' is our foundation word. It is the key to "The Obstacle Course"; it is the key to life. We are all learning things constantly, yet we only choose to recognize the learning process when we are in classes in school. Even then, as you, my friends, know, we tend to complicate matters by adding some structure and form to the process – things like syllabuses, published reading lists, and... yes, believe-it-or-not, grades!"

"Remember when you were all children?" he asked. "Wasn't it FUN when you first learned the names of people, places, and things? Wasn't it FUN when someone asked you what color something was and you guessed... and you were right? Wasn't it fun when words in books started to make sense and symbols that you learned were numbers started to add up to other numbers... and you understood it all?"

Heads started nodding in agreement.

"For most people, learning is FUN!" he exclaimed. "For many people, learning continues to be fun – even till the day they die – because we, as human beings, have a natural curiosity about things. We gain a sense of excitement from understanding the world around us and from using our understanding to influence our individual and collective relationships with society and our environment."

"Unfortunately," Dr. Acton continued, "Many of us get turned off by the structure and form of the learning process itself and by the many pressures that are often placed by well-meaning people upon us. We tend to rebel, and 'learning' somehow becomes no more fun."

More heads nodded in agreement.

"Now," he continued, "Our first couple of classes may have seemed a bit odd to some of you... no, probably all of you... but I hope I have made a few things clear."

Dr. Acton then wrote on the board:

(1) If you want this course to be helpful to you, open your mind to it.

(2) 'Uncertainty' stops many people from accomplishing things; You did not allow obstacles to block your path, and you are learning here today.

(3) Sometimes we all need to think.

(4) Sometimes we need to ask.

(5) Sometimes we need to ask again.

(6) We must focus our minds to learn that which we are seeking to learn.

(7)   We must learn by earnest, thoughtful action.

(8)   We must not let interruptions block our course.

(9)   Leave your worries at the door; you will do well.

(10) 'Learn' is our foundation word. It is the key to the "Obstacle Course". It is the key to life.

(11) At the core of learning is listening.

(12) For many people, the learning process itself becomes an obstacle.

(13) Remember, learning is "FUN"!

We sat astonished as Dr. Acton filled the entire blackboard with these 13 messages. Why 13? Probably coincidence, but after these first few classes, we weren't so sure. We were amazed that the old man wrote everything down, one point after another, without hesitation... and without any notes!

Furthermore, he insisted that we not copy the information from the board. "There's plenty of time left for the class. Read it to yourselves over and over again until you're sure you have the gist of each message," he said. "See you next week!"

Then he swiftly grabbed his portfolio from the desk and walked quickly to the door.

"Oh, it's jammed shut!" he said.

The "trick" worked. Got him! It was difficult to conceal our smiles, but he probably thought we were just surprised, too. It was funny.

What would Dr. Acton do now? Boy, were we curious... we were stuck in the room, too!

Chapter 6

"It seems we have a little challenge here," the wise old Acton remarked. "The door seems to be jammed from the other side. This is terrific!"

"Terrific?" called a voice from the middle of the third row. "We're stuck! This is terrible!"

"Terrible?" questioned Dr. Acton. "Nonsense! This is terrific! I've got a real live captive audience! You cannot escape from learning something tonight! Although I wasn't planning on covering so much material this soon, we'll take advantage of this opportunity to have a 'doubleheader'!"

So, we get locked in, and that's good because it's double-header time! The looks on faces throughout the room were incredulous. I wondered what the old man ate for breakfast.

"Please don't erase the board yet," came a plea from a corner of the room.

"Don't worry, you'll have a few minutes more," assured Dr. Acton. "Just be sure YOU don't erase the board. You know, some people erase the board before they ever learn what was on it."

For a short time, the class silently stared at the blackboard, each of us reading and then re-reading the messages. It didn't seem like it would be hard to remember any of the things that were listed. Dr. Acton had been quite emphatic when he had first mentioned them in class, and the mental repetition now seemed to bind them into memory.

The study drill complete, the teacher methodically erased the entire blackboard, taking care not to miss a mark.

"Let's talk about another word," he said, writing the word A-T-T-I-T-U-D-E. "Attitude"

"What is a person's attitude?" he asked.

Hands raised. He called upon Nancy.

"It's the way someone acts or feels about things," she answered.

"Can you elaborate?" he inquired.

"Well, yes," she replied. "It's the manner in which they think about things."

"Just a moment… You're talking about how someone acts, feels, and thinks about things? Am I right?" he asked.

"Yes," said Nancy.

"What kind of things? Can you give an example?" the teacher asked.

"Well, like what just happened earlier, Dr. Acton. Your attitude was unbelievable!" she exclaimed.

"How's that?" he asked.

"You simply didn't let the jammed door bother you… I still can't believe what you did… You viewed it as something wonderful!" she said.

"So that was my attitude, wasn't it? How should I have viewed it, in your opinion?" he asked.

"I think most people would have viewed it as a problem and perhaps gotten upset," Nancy said.

"Oh, if I had done that, what would that have solved, and what would I have taught you?" he asked.

"I guess it wouldn't have solved much, but we would have learned how angry you can get!" she said with a smile. Her comment got a few laughs from the audience.

"But that is not what this class is about, and that is not the type of role model I am trying to be for you," Dr. Acton remarked. "So, I made a decision to have a positive attitude about what happened and to view our predicament as a challenge rather than a problem. See, a 'challenge' to most people seems like a contest that can be won; a 'problem' seems like an obstacle that is insurmountable. It may sound like wordplay, but it is all about one's attitude."

"You chose your attitude, Dr. Acton," Nancy echoed.

"Yes, I did," he replied. "We all can choose the attitudes we wish to bring to situations we confront each day. Every one of us can choose. Rather than getting frustrated about the door being jammed and seeing it as roadblock to where I wanted to go, I looked at what happened as an opportunity to move forward in another direction I wanted to go – teaching the class more information."

"But the door is still jammed," reminded John.

"So it is!" said Dr. Acton. "But, rather than panic, we will deal with the challenge appropriately. The janitor will be passing by soon, and he will surely be able to help. Class, I would not worry about the door anymore. We will still get to go home tonight."

"How much does one's attitude affect how he deals with obstacles, Dr. Acton?" came a question from Bill, a generally shy fellow who, paradoxically, always sits in the front row.

"It affects a person immensely," the doctor said. "Your attitude towards something will help determine whether, for you, it is an obstacle at all and whether you believe it can easily be overcome or not. What appears to be an obstacle in life for one person may not be for another; similarly, the degree of difficulty that an obstacle may present varies from individual to individual."

He continued, "One person may panic in response to a particular situation, thereby making his or her obstacle seem extremely difficult. Thinking calmly and rationally, however, that same person may not perceive much difficulty at all."

I came to the conclusion that there must not have been any great significance to having exactly 13 messages on the blackboard earlier. Onto the board came several more:

(14) Attitude is the way someone acts, feels, or thinks about persons, places, or things.

(15) People usually view "challenges" as contests that they can win; they perceive "problems" more as insurmountable obstacles.

(16) You can choose your attitudes towards dealing with situations.

(17) A person's attitude immensely affects how he or she deals with obstacles. One's attitude itself can become an obstacle.

As he finished his writing, Dr. Acton glanced toward the door. "Well, it looks like our friend the janitor noticed our little jam. Perhaps someone on the outside let him in on the ruse?"

I never saw so many brick red faces in my life!

"Before you leave, be sure to review the messages I've written," he instructed us.

With a cheerful "Goodnight!" and a huge grin, Dr. Acton grabbed his portfolio, quickly walked to the door, turned the knob, pushed it open... and disappeared.

Neal R. Voron

Chapter 7

Somehow, I was beginning to feel that perhaps we could learn a few things from strange, old Dr. Acton. Although he was much different than any other teacher whose class I had taken, he seemed to be a real teacher in the truest sense of the word.

The next class began promptly at 7 p.m., after Dr. Acton took just a split second to check the door as he strode into the room. No new faces were in attendance, but all 35 of us from last week were still aboard. A quick survey of the room showed 18 women and 17 men.

The teacher carefully stood his portfolio atop the desk, smiled broadly, and asked to no one in particular, "No need for a doubleheader today?"

The sound of dozens of bodies shifting in their chairs echoed throughout the room. "One never knows!" came a snicker from the back row.

"That's true!" Dr. Acton replied. "One NEVER knows! One never KNOWS exactly what will happen; we only think we know what will happen! Isn't that so?"

"Well, I don't think that's so," answered John, quickly putting the old man to the test. "If you take a penny and toss it into the air, we all know it will fall to the ground. We don't just think that; we know it."

"And how do you know it?" Dr. Acton asked. "And please tell me your name, young man!"

23

John seemed taken aback, perhaps wondering if he had stuck his neck out too far. "Well, er... Sir... Dr. Acton, Sir, my name's John – John Archer. I hope I haven't offended you with my reply. That was not my intent."

"Son, you worry where you need not. Far from taking offense, I am glad you have the courage to speak your mind, John," the wise man counseled. "But, again, I ask, 'How do we know the penny will fall to the ground?"

John hesitated.

"From past experience," I murmured.

"That's right!" John exclaimed. "We know from past experience and from the laws of gravity. What goes up must come down!"

"Oh, I see," was Dr. Acton's response. He reached into his pocket and produced a penny, which he promptly tossed into the air with an underhand flip. The penny rapidly angled upward and, upon reaching its apex, descended swiftly toward the ground. But an interesting thing happened along the way: it landed in Acton's open portfolio atop the desk.

"Good shot, huh, Class?" the wise man remarked. "John, didn't you say that if I toss a penny into the air it will fall to the ground? This penny didn't quite make it all the way!"

Dr. Acton reiterated his earlier statement, "One never KNOWS exactly what will happen; we only think we know what will happen."

Nobody disagreed this time. He was right. The penny did not reach the ground. Our past experiences enabled us to make a prediction that seemed reasonable and dependable, but we did not – and perhaps could not – anticipate the influence of variables like the angle of his toss and the presence of an obstacle (the portfolio).

The teacher did not stop there, however. "Lest anyone accuse me of playing with words with that example, let us examine the situation again. For many, many years, man's past experiences did indeed enable us to predict that what goes up must come down. But, with our exploration of outer space, we gained knowledge about a condition where weightlessness exists. In 'zero gravity' – as the condition is now known – our tossed penny would float in the air! In our wildest imaginations, few of us would have ever considered the possibility of that happening."

"My friends," the doctor gently reassured us, "We only think we know what the future will bring."

He turned toward the blackboard and wrote:

(18) One never KNOWS exactly what will happen.

(19) We only think we know what will happen.

(20) Our past experiences enable us to make predictions about future events that seem reasonable and dependable, but we cannot be certain predictions will come true.

(21) We cannot always anticipate the influence of variables.

He then paused for a moment and turned toward Bill.

"If we cannot always anticipate the influence of variables, can we control them?" he asked him.

"I guess we could try," Bill surmised.

"Can we control all of them?" the teacher asked, pointing to me for a reply.

"Maybe most," I said. "But probably not all, being that we cannot always anticipate their influence."

"You're sounding good," Dr. Acton said, nodding toward Bill and me.

Then Nancy asked, "Dr. Acton, how can we control all variables in a given situation if we don't know what all the variables that affect the situation are?"

"That's a good question, young woman!" he replied. "How can we control them if we don't know what they are?" he repeated, throwing her question back at the class.

John offered a suggestion, "Control those that you are aware of as best as you can. Go forward into the future with an open mind about the influences of unknown variables."

"Good, Good!!!" the teacher interjected. "Now you are all really thinking this through!"

A hand raised high in the back of the room. "Dr. Acton," a young man named Jim inquired, "What are we talking about? We're going on and on about predictions and variables and control... What do these things have to do with dealing with obstacles?"

"Just have some patience, son," Acton replied. "Think about what we have discussed. In time, you will see... it will make more sense."

The old man returned to the blackboard and wrote:

(22) We can try to control variables.

(23) We probably cannot control all variables; we don't know what all of them are.

(24) We can try to control the variables we are aware of as best as we can.

(25) We can go forward into the future with an open mind about the influences of unknown variables.

"Well, I guess there will be no need for a doubleheader today," Dr. Acton said as he finished his writing and almost ran out of blackboard space. "Make sure you spend a few minutes reviewing the notes. Oh, and one more thing…"

He reached into his pocket and produced another penny. "Anyone care to predict what will happen to this penny?" he asked.

There were a lot of nods indicating "no", and no one offered a guess. The old man waited a moment and then gave an underhand flip to this coin. Up, up in the air it went high above the desk. Then it came down, down – right into his open portfolio.

With a big smile, but without another word, the wise guy grabbed the bag, quickly strode out of the room, and disappeared down the hallway.

What a man! He certainly made it clear that – one way or another – we were going to get our two cents' worth!

Neal R. Voron

Chapter 8

The clock struck 7 p.m. It seemed like everyone was in class, and a quick count indicated all 35 students were present. But everyone was not there. Dr. Acton was missing!

The teacher's late! How about that? The whole class was pretty much surprised because Dr. Acton was always extremely punctual, so in control, on top of everything... or so it had seemed. I know I had been so impressed by his punctuality that I actually looked forward to seeing him stride into the room precisely at 7 p.m. I had come to know that I could count on him to do that... or, at least I thought I had.

A low murmur of excitement buzzed throughout the room as we individually and collectively realized our idealized leader was... no doubt about it... late! At 7:03 p.m., the noise died down a bit, but the old man still wasn't there.

Slowly, the seconds and minutes ticked away... 7:05... 7:06... 7:07... 7:08...

"Where is he?" Jim exclaimed, aloud and to no one in particular.

"This certainly isn't like him," added John. "I hope there's nothing wrong!"

"Maybe he got stuck in the bathroom!" came a male voice from the rear.

That comment got a few laughs, and I couldn't help but smile myself.

"Maybe someone should check," Nancy suggested. A quick glance at her indicated she was not joking.

"Are you serious?" Jim asked. "Then go ahead!" he told her. That got a few more laughs, but not nearly as many and certainly not from me. Nancy was not impressed at all.

"I'll go," offered Bill. He got up and left the room to check the Men's Room.

"I'm going, too!" said Jim. "But, I'm leaving! He's not going to show tonight... you're all wasting your time!"

He got up and grabbed his jacket. Two of his pals got up, too. They left the room shaking their heads, obviously feeling they had wasted their time coming to class tonight.

I looked at the clock. It was only 7:12. The rest of the class decided to wait a little longer.

Less than a minute later, in walked Bill with a smile on his face. Striding in behind him, also smiling, was Dr. Acton! And he was shortly followed by Jim and friends.

"See, he was in the bathroom!" Nancy proudly boasted to our surprised class.

"The bathroom?" Dr. Acton inquired, looking puzzled as he hoisted his portfolio onto the desk. "Is that where you and your buddies were, Jim?"

Jim's face turned scarlet. "Er... yes, Dr. Acton!" he replied, fooling nobody. He turned his face sharply away as he walked past Nancy to his seat.

"Dr. Acton, are you okay?" John asked.

"I am fine, thank you, John!" the old man responded with enthusiasm, seemingly delighted with the personal concern afforded him.

Then, addressing the group, Dr. Acton said, "I am so proud of all of you! You are indeed committed to 'staying the course', I should say! Please pardon the pun!... You did not let my lateness block you from getting an evening's education."

"We knew you would be here, Dr. Acton," I offered.

"Oh, did you?" he asked.

"Yes, you haven't miss a class yet," I said. "And you're usually very punctual. We knew you would be here."

"Thanks for the confidence!" he said. "But, weren't you a bit surprised when I wasn't here precisely at 7 p.m.? Didn't you think you knew I would show up then? In fact, you probably predicted in your mind that I would."

"Well, yes," I admitted.

"Then you were probably disappointed – and wrong – today, weren't you?" he replied.

"Yes, I guess I was wrong and didn't really know you would show up precisely at 7," I told him. "But I'm not disappointed in you for being late – just surprised."

"Oh, my friend, this conversation is not at all about personalities," he advised. "It is about reinforcement and providing all of you with another example... one that you can relate to."

"An example?" Jim interjected. "An example of what?"

"Son, have patience, and I will explain!" the old man retorted. "It is an example of what we were talking about in our last meeting! One never KNOWS exactly what will happen. We only think we know what will happen! These concepts are important, and I must make sure that you are prepared to deal with them."

"You all expected me to appear at 7 o'clock," he continued. "When I did not, all sorts of possibilities existed about where I could be and why. And all sorts of possibilities existed about how each of you and all of you, collectively as a group, could have responded to my not being here."

"Jim, you had said you wanted to know what the things we have been talking about have to do with dealing with obstacles. I suggest that you – all of you – pay close attention," Dr. Acton instructed.

"So, were you in the bathroom?" Jim asked. His comment elicited a few snickers.

"In fact, young man, no," came the reply. I was shocked that Dr. Acton even acknowledged Jim. "I was in the classroom next door."

"You were in the classroom next door!" Jim exclaimed. "Why?" he asked.

"Well, although that could be considered a rather personal question, I'll explain," the teacher said.

We couldn't wait. Why was he late? What was he doing in the classroom next door? And, why was he going to explain it to us? He certainly didn't have to.

His explanation astounded us.

"I was simply waiting to determine your response," he said.

"Waiting to determine our response!" Jim exclaimed. He was flabbergasted. "Were you willing to wait all night?"

"Perhaps!" Dr. Acton replied. "Were you, Jim?"

"No!" Jim said. "No way!"

"I did not think so," Acton declared. "But then you would have missed the opportunity for an evening's education. Your classmates were wise enough not to panic, not to jump to conclusions, not to leave without still trying to attain their goal of being educated. They reassessed their situation and thought to send Bill to find me. It worked, and I am impressed. You are all to be congratulated."

Nancy beamed. Bill smiled. Jim kept his mouth shut.

Dr. Acton continued, "The possibilities that existed tonight at 7 p.m. existed irrespective of your past knowledge and experience, and regardless of your predictions. You could not have reasonably expected that I would have done what I did. What I did was throw an obstacle in your path to learning. The important thing was how you viewed that obstacle and how you responded to it. You did not let the obstacle block your opportunity."

Acton had done it again! Was he clever, or what? Just when we thought we could expect certain things, he did the unexpected! Actually, though, looking back... most things he's done have been unexpected...

"Class," the teacher continued, "Be careful not to misunderstand what I am saying. Predictions can be helpful.

Reasonable expectations are often prudent. Just make sure you do not get stuck on them."

"Dr. Acton," John interrupted, "What do you mean by not getting 'stuck' on them?"

"I mean be flexible enough in your thinking to realize that habits can be broken, plans can change, new ideas can take root, a tornado can literally blow whatever you expected away," he replied. "Be open-minded to a myriad of possibilities surrounding everything that happens – and everything that does not happen... everything you do, and everything you do not do. The key is to adapt to whatever occurs in a way that helps you achieve your goals."

He continued, "Tonight, as on any other night, there existed the possibility that I could be late to class... and I was! Next time, who knows? I may be early!"

"Now, let us look at 'reasonable expectations' another way... in terms of success and failure," the teacher suggested.

"People often measure their personal successes by how well they handle challenges that they can reasonably expect. That is easy!" he said. "For example, for our last meeting the class was reasonably expecting me to arrive at precisely 7 p.m... I did, and the class was easily successful in reaching its goal of getting an evening's education."

"However," he continued, "It is more difficult to confront unexpected challenges, such as when I arrived late tonight. You have to think, you may have to be creative – you may even have to go to the bathroom like our friend Bill was about to do – to adapt to the situation in a way that helps you achieve your goals."

"Tonight," he elaborated, "Bill's effort was successful, and everyone benefited from it. Sometimes, though, you may adapt in a way that will fail. For instance, you could have all left for the evening without waiting for me to arrive and without trying to find me. If I would have remained in the classroom next door and allowed you to leave, you would have adapted to the situation in a way that would have failed to achieve your original goal of getting an evening's education."

The next statement he said surprised me.

"But failure can often be good!" Dr. Acton said.

"Good?" I asked, not realizing I had spoken aloud.

"Yes, I said 'Good'," Dr. Acton replied. "If you try doing something to achieve a goal, but you 'fail' and are not successful in achieving the goal, you may still have made progress toward the goal. If you do not try, and, by trying, risk failure, you would not make that progress. Also, if you do not try, you will surely fail in reaching your goal anyway."

"For example, Bill tried to find me and made progress by his effort. Had nobody tried and had the class left, you would not have made that progress. Now, if I had not called Bill over when I saw him headed toward the Men's Room and had he not found me at the Men's Room, he would have reported back to the class that I could not be found there. Then you would at least have had that additional information prior to making your next decision about what to do because I had not arrived," he said. "See?"

He continued, "There is a lot that can be learned from failure, and that knowledge is often worth the price of the effort. It may be just what you need to ultimately be successful in achieving the original goal or another goal."

35

"So, Dr. Acton, are you saying that we should look at dealing with unexpected challenges and confronting potential failure as personal growth opportunities?" Nancy asked.

"Yes, and you can look at 'expected challenges' that way, too," the wise man replied. "Strive for success. Focus on your goals. Turn potential negatives into positives. Adapt your strategy, if necessary, to handle both the expected and the unexpected. Make every effort work for you. That's how you climb towards where you want to be."

He walked to the blackboard and began writing:

(26) All sorts of happening possibilities exist regardless of reasonable expectation based upon past habits or experience.

(27) All sorts of adaptation possibilities exist to handle both expected and unexpected challenges.

(28) Someone who holds an opportunity for you may be watching to see if you will let obstacles stand in the way of your goals.

***(29) Beware: someone who does not want you to reach your goals may put obstacles in your way to try to block you.

(30) When confronted with an unexpected challenge, be wise enough not to panic, not to jump to conclusions, not to wantonly abandon your goal.

(31) How you view obstacles and how you respond to them is important.

(32) Predictions can be helpful, but do not get stuck on them!

(33) Be flexible and open-minded in your thinking.

(34) The key is to adapt to whatever occurs in a way that helps you achieve your goals.

(35) Achieving success by handling challenges you can reasonably expect is easy; It is more difficult to confront unexpected challenges.

Dr. Acton was writing so much, he had to write on the blackboard at the back of the room, too:

(36) You may have to be creative to adapt to a situation.

(37) Sometimes you may adapt in a way that will fail; But failure can often be good!

(38) Trying and failing may still lead to progress toward a goal.

(39) If you do not try, you will surely fail.

(40) There is a lot to be learned from failure; That knowledge is often worth the price of the effort – it may help you achieve your goals.

(41) Look at dealing with expected & unexpected challenges and confronting potential failure as personal growth opportunities!

(42) Strive for success.

(43) Focus on your goals.

(44) Turn potential negatives into positives.

(45) Make every effort work for you.

"I guess that's about it for now," the old man said as he used up the last bit of blackboard space in the room. He walked to the front and turned around to face the class.

"Pay special attention to Number 29," he advised. "I threw that one in for you to think about. Spend some time reviewing the whole list before you leave. It will be worth it," he assured us.

"Goodnight!" Dr. Acton said, as he grabbed his bag. "See you next class!"

Within seconds, he was gone. About two dozen pens and notebooks quickly opened and the writing began. Nancy announced she had previously written the first 25 notes if anybody wanted to jot them down, too. We must have been nuts. There were lots of takers.

Dr. Acton himself may have the greatest mind in the world, but, as he did, we wanted the material he presented to make a lasting impression. That was our goal, and we weren't going to let his style block our way.

Chapter 9

Dr. Acton was early for our next class, arriving even before Bill and Nancy, who usually were the earliest arrivals. I first noticed he was there when I saw his portfolio standing atop the desk next to a box marked "fragile". Then I saw he was busy doing some writing on the blackboard at the back of the room. He had written the words "forward" and "backward".

"Good evening!" he greeted us. "Kindly turn your chairs around facing the back," he instructed.

We obliged, curious about what the old man had on his mind this day.

"Are we looking forward or backward, my friends?" he asked.

Good question, I thought. "Does it make a difference?" I murmured.

"We will see," he replied to me. "Does anyone have a thought about it?"

"Forward!" John replied. Some heads nodded in agreement.

"Backward!" countered Jim. Other heads nodded.

"They're both right!" I thought, not realizing I said the words aloud.

"How many of us have eyes on both sides of our head?" Dr. Acton responded, stretching his neck out as his eyes scanned the room for an answer.

"None of us, Dr. Acton," said John.

"None of us," Jim agreed. "I still think we're looking backward."

"All of us," I offered in a low voice.

"What was that?" Doctor Acton asked. I couldn't believe he didn't hear me. "Did you say 'All of us', my friend?"

"Yes, all of us," I replied.

Heads turned toward me in puzzlement. What weird looks they gave me!

Dr. Acton just smiled.

"Who is right?" he finally asked the class.

John and Jim each got votes of support, but only indirectly from me.

"We all are," I offered. That response elicited more looks of puzzlement.

Dr. Acton seemed pleased. "Could you explain?" he asked.

"It's all a matter of perspective, Dr. Acton," I said. "And semantics."

"Please continue," he requested.

"John is correct in saying we're looking forward because we are looking straight ahead at you – our focal point – without turning our head backwards... But, Jim is also right if we choose to consider that, semantically, we are looking at the back of the room. We are looking back-ward, toward the back," I explained.

"Interesting!" Dr. Acton replied. My classmates seemed somewhat impressed. "But how can you say we all have eyes on both sides of our head?" he asked.

"That's all a matter of perspective, too," I answered. "We each have an eye on the right side of our head and an eye on the left side of our head."

"Ohhh!" came voices from throughout the room.

"I think everyone else was only thinking about the front and the back of the head," I surmised. "If that's how we wish to define 'sides of the head', then John and Jim were right. So, in a way, we were all right."

"Very interesting perspective! Thank you for sharing it," Dr. Acton excitedly replied. "I like that word 'perspective'," he said. "Does everybody see how one's perspective can affect one's perception of what is correct? Does everybody see how perspectives and perceptions can differ?"

Heads nodded in agreement. I felt vindicated.

He continued, "This is important to know because the perspective in which you view things and the perception you form about them are factors which affect your interactions with them."

"For example," he explained. "Suppose you knew 10 people applied for a job you were interested in. Would you apply?

If you viewed the 10 other applicants as an insurmountable amount of competition, you might not apply. However, if you viewed the situation as your having a one-in-11 – or better, because of your qualifications – chance, then you might apply. Actually, objectively, a one-in-eleven chance at anything is not too bad, especially if you compare it to the odds of winning a lottery."

"Anyhow," the wise man continued, "I am teaching you tonight at the back of the room simply to introduce the notion that things can be viewed differently and done differently if you allow yourself to break patterns or to look beyond the familiar."

He wrote on the board:

(46) One's perspective can affect one's perception of what is correct.

(47) Perspectives and perceptions can differ.

(48) The perspective in which you view things and the perception you form about them are factors which affect your interactions with them.

(49) You can view things differently and do things differently if you allow yourself to break patterns or to look beyond the familiar.

Dr. Acton turned around and looked at the class. "Things are not always as they appear, either," he declared. "Jim, would you mind bringing me the box on the desk? Be careful, it is fragile."

Jim brought the old man the box. "Would you mind standing here as a volunteer?" Dr. Acton asked him. Jim obliged with a smile.

We were curious… What was Acton up to?

He had Jim stand facing the blackboard, with his back to the class. Then he took out a large, square glass tile and held it about two feet in front of Jim's face. It looked clear, like a window.

"What is this?" Acton asked him.

"A clear piece of glass – a glass tile," Jim replied.

"Are you sure?" the teacher asked.

"A clear piece of glass?" Dr. Acton asked.

"Yes," Jim replied.

Then Acton asked him to look again. This time, he flipped the glass over. This side was shiny, like a mirror, and we could see Jim's reflection.

"Oh, it's a mirror!" Jim said.

"Now, Jim, what is it – a clear piece of glass or a mirror?" Dr. Acton asked.

"I guess it's both," Jim answered.

"It did not look that way at first, did it?" Acton inquired.

"No," Jim conceded.

"Things are not always as they appear," the teacher again told the class.

"Jim, please turn toward the class. Nancy, what does Jim's shirt say?" Dr. Acton asked.

Jim turned around, looking embarrassed.

"It says 'ox'," Nancy said, smiling.

"Is that so?" Dr. Acton asked. "Jim, I did not mean to embarrass you. Please turn around and hold the mirror out in front of you."

Jim turned around and held out the mirror. Dr. Acton walked behind him.

"It does not look like it spells the word 'ox' to me," he told the class. "In fact, I am not sure I know what 'x-o' means!"

Acton reminded us still another time, "Things are not always as they appear."

The old man looked at Jim for a moment. "Jim, I appreciate your help with this demonstration, and I really did not mean to embarrass you… so, if you will help me just a little more, I will give you a chance to get back at me, okay?"

Jim's face lit up. "Okay!" he replied. Acton sure knew how to keep people's attention!

The teacher went over to the box and took out another tile that was covered by cloth on both sides. Acton gave the tile to Jim and stood where Jim had with his back to the class.

"Okay, hold the mirror in front of me and lift up the cloth, Jim!" he instructed. Jim obliged.

The class roared with laughter! Acton's face in the mirror looked as fat as a pig's, and his nose seemed elongated! It was one of those 'trick' mirrors that distort your image. Jim quickly gave Acton the mirror to hold so he could see what the commotion was about.

"That is great!" Jim declared. "You're okay, old man!"

Acton smiled.

"What's on the other side, Dr. Acton?" Jim asked.

Acton was a pretty good sport. He flipped the tile over and lifted up the cloth. It was hilarious! This time, his face was elongated and his nose was extra wide. The class roared again with laughter.

Jim patted the old man on the back and returned to his seat. Acton put the tiles in the box and then went to the blackboard. He wrote:

(50) Things are not always as they appear.

"That's enough fun for tonight," Acton said, as he picked up the box. "Make sure you spend time reviewing the material."

He walked to the front of the room and grabbed his portfolio. "Oh, I have a homework assignment for you," he said.

Homework? Panic spread throughout the room. He never told us there would be homework!

"Write down one obstacle you would like to overcome. Just one sentence, please," he instructed. "Be sure to bring it to class next time." He smiled at us, turned, and walked out of the room.

Somehow I thought we could handle that assignment.

Neal R. Voron

Chapter 10

Before Dr. Acton arrived for the next class, everyone started talking about the homework assignment and what they had written. That is, everyone except Jim. He didn't do the assignment. "I can't do homework," he said. "That's my obstacle!"

Dr. Acton arrived promptly at 7:00 p.m. and told us there would be no need to turn our chairs around this time. He tossed his portfolio onto the desk, smiled, rubbed his hands together, and then asked for our homework.

We passed our assignment sheets to him, and he half-sat against the side of the desk to read our single-sentence roadblocks. The class was anxious as he quickly read the 34 sentences silently to himself.

The wise man looked up and scanned the room, finally focusing his eyes upon Jim.

"Jim," he asked, "Do you have a problem doing homework?"

We tried to restrain ourselves from laughing.

"Yes, sir," Jim replied. "I just can't do it."

Nancy burst out laughing.

"You can't?" Dr. Acton asked. "Do you mean cannot or will not? Surely you can write down a single sentence on a piece of paper."

"Well, I can do it, but I just can't get myself to do it," Jim answered. "You know what I mean?"

"Yes, I believe I do," Acton told him. "Something seems to be limiting – or blocking – you from doing homework. Is that right?"

"That's right!" Jim replied.

"This could be serious," the teacher informed him. "Class," he asked us, "Do you have any ideas about what is 'blocking' Jim?"

The replies came swiftly:

"He's lazy!" said one student.

"He doesn't think he has to do it," said another.

"He's testing you, Dr. Acton!" said a third.

Jim smiled with embarrassment. All three suggested reasons sounded like they could be right.

Dr. Acton interjected, "I think that perhaps Jim has self-imposed some limitations. What do you think, Jim?"

"You might be right, Dr. Acton," he conceded.

"Jim, self-imposed limitations are malleable. That means you can change them. They are also expendable. You can get rid of them – if you decide to," Acton said. "I do not care if you do your homework. I am not disappointed. The question is, 'Do you care if you reach your goals for this course?' Your goals are your goals, and that's okay. I just thought that perhaps you would want to take advantage of every single learning opportunity. I guess I was wrong."

"How could I have learned more by writing a single sentence about an obstacle?" Jim asked.

"Write one, and you will see," the wise old Acton answered. "Go ahead!"

Jim quickly scribbled onto a sheet of paper:

"I can't do homework.
– Jim"

He walked up to Dr. Acton and handed it to him.

"That's good!" said Acton. "There! You just learned that you can do homework! Now, next time just do it at home!"

We were awestruck. How did Dr. Acton get such a knack for turning nonsense to sense? His shrewdness was only exceeded by his ability to utilize his shrewdness spontaneously.

But if we were awestruck by how the old man handled Jim, we were absolutely flabbergasted by what he did next. He started ripping up the homework papers! We couldn't believe it! Rip, rip, rip! Methodically, he was tearing them in half, then in half again, then in half again, into small pieces!

We watched the old man in astonishment as he made a little mound of confetti on the desk.

"What are you doing?" asked John.

"First, I acknowledged your homework by reading the obstacles you listed – we will discuss some of what you wrote later. Then I destroyed your obstacles as much as I could by myself," Dr. Acton replied.

"But you really can't destroy them, Dr. Acton!" Jim interjected.

"Listen: I destroyed them as much as I could by myself," Dr. Acton repeated.

"That means you can't really destroy our obstacles for us, Dr. Acton, doesn't it?" asked John.

"Only you can destroy your own obstacles, John, and only you can destroy your own obstacles, Jim," Acton told them. "I can only teach you to recognize, to understand, to think, to apply. You all must confront the obstacles that confront you if you seek to get past them."

"So, why did you tear up the sheets, Dr. Acton?" asked Nancy.

"Young woman," he replied. "I did it simply to illustrate the little power others have over your personal situations. You are the one with power over your situation. I can only try to help. I must say, though, from looking at the obstacles listed, some of you could destroy them by doing little more than what I did by tearing the papers."

"How's that?" asked Mike.

"By viewing them differently. Do not think of them as 'obstacles'. Think of them as 'obfuscations'," Acton said.

Boy, did the old man like semantics! "There's nothing like playing with words," I thought aloud.

"Oh, my friend, this is not just semantics," the teacher assured me. "Let us talk about this some more. But first, let us review what we have spoken about."

He walked to the blackboard and wrote:

(51) Is it that you cannot or will not overcome obstacles?

(52) Self-imposed limitations are malleable. That means you can change them. They are also expendable. You can get rid of them if you decide to.

(53) Do you care if you reach your goals?

(54) Your goals are your goals.

(55) Only you can destroy your own obstacles.

(56) You must confront your obstacles if you seek to get past them.

(57) Others have little power over your personal situation. YOU are the one with the power.

(58) Viewing obstacles differently could help you destroy them. (View obstacles as obfuscations.)

For some reason, I thought this class might last longer tonight than on previous nights. I was right; this class had only just begun.

Chapter 11

"Okay, everybody please sit up straight," Dr. Acton instructed us. "We are going to try a little exercise. Everyone look straight ahead toward the blackboard... Pay close attention... Do not move your head... Think about what you see directly in front of you... Okay, relax."

"Now," he continued, "I am going to ask each of you six in the front row to tell the class what you saw. John, you tell us first, and then each of you follow in order."

John said he saw only the blackboard.

Bill said he saw only the blackboard.

Kelly said she saw only the blackboard.

Sue said she saw Dr. Acton and the blackboard.

Tom said he saw the desk and the blackboard.

Cathy said she saw only the blackboard.

"Okay, second row, what did you see?" Acton asked.

Nancy said she saw John's head and the blackboard.

Kim said she saw Bill's head and the blackboard.

I said I saw Kelly's head and the blackboard.

Renee said she saw Sue's head, Dr. Acton and the blackboard.

Joe said he saw Tom's head, the desk and the blackboard.

Mike said he saw Cathy's head and the blackboard.

Jim in the back grew impatient. "What's this all about?" he asked the teacher.

"You'll soon see," Dr. Acton assured him. "Okay, those of you in the back four rows, is it safe to assume that all of you saw the back of somebody's head and the blackboard and that some of you also saw either me or the desk?"

"Yes!" was the collective response.

"Fine," Dr. Acton said. "Now, everyone shut your eyes. Go ahead, right now. I want all of you to imagine that you are looking only at the blackboard. Again, starting with John, tell everyone what you see."

John said, "The blackboard." Bill said, "The blackboard." Everyone in the front two rows said only "the blackboard" except Mike, who said "Cathy and the blackboard."

Dr. Acton asked the rest of the class whether they all saw the blackboard. They said they did. He asked if anyone besides Mike saw anything (or anyone) else besides the blackboard. No one said they did.

"Now, what is this about?" Jim asked again.

"Okay, okay," the old man replied. "This is about obstacles and perceptions, about perspectives and visualizations, about what obstacles are and what they are not. And this is about each of ours' ability to deal with obstacles."

"What just happened?" he asked us, without pausing for a reply. "At first, with your eyes fully open, most of you saw

54

what we will call obstacles blocking at least some of your view of the blackboard."

"Then, with your eyes closed," he continued, "all but one of you were able to visualize the blackboard without the obstacles. Quite amazing, is it not?"

"Visualization can be a powerful tool that you can use to help see beyond obstacles," Dr. Acton said. "Remember what we discussed in an earlier class: the perspective in which you view things and the perception you form about them are factors which affect your interactions with them. Visualization can help you stay focused on your goals and may also help you see another path to reaching them."

The old man turned toward Cathy and put his hand under his chin as if deliberating about whether to ask her a question. Instead, he asked Mike to bear with him and forgive him for singling him out as an example. "Cathy," he asked, "Do you have any thoughts about Mike's stated inability to visualize the blackboard without seeing your head?"

Eyes from throughout the room zeroed in on both Cathy and Mike for their reactions. They both were blushing, slightly embarrassed at the attention and surprised by Dr. Acton's question.

I don't know what old man Acton expected Cathy to say, and I don't know what I expected her to say either, but I sure didn't expect her to say what she said!

With a big smile, Cathy turned toward Mike and declared to the class, "Actually, I'm very flattered!"

Heads turned quickly towards Mike, who seemed quite surprised, but pleased. Then Dr. Acton asked another strange question, "Mike, are you now able to visualize the goal that your homework 'obstacle' was blocking?"

"Yes!" Mike replied enthusiastically. He looked straight ahead at Cathy, glanced at Dr. Acton momentarily, and then thanked Cathy and asked her if she would like to join him after class for a milkshake!

We were puzzled, but Mike, Cathy, and Dr. Acton all seemed happy. What had happened?

"Mike, may I have your permission to explain?" the teacher asked. Mike nodded yes.

"Mike had written for his 'homework obstacle' that he was afraid to ask Cathy for a date because he felt she might reject him," Dr. Acton informed us. "Apparently, with our little turn of events – namely, Cathy's positive comment – Mike was able to visualize his goal as a reality and mustered the courage to confront his fear of asking her."

Cathy and Mike blushed again, but they seemed happy.

"Congratulations, you two!" Dr. Acton offered. In the name of teaching, he had become a matchmaker! "See how perceptions and visualizations can help overcome obstacles?" he asked us.

Mike now had a question. "Dr. Acton, did you seriously expect Cathy to give the response she gave to your question?"

"Of course not, son. I simply thought she might say something like, 'Some people just have difficulty with visualizations,'" he replied. "She would have been right if she had said that, you know. It is difficult for some people to visualize their goals clearly without seeing roadblocks."

"If you ever have difficulty with your visualizations," Acton suggested, "Practice them, concentrating on your goal and on eliminating any obstacles that may present themselves."

"Now, my friends," he cautioned, "I am not suggesting that you will not have to deal with any obstacles. I am just emphasizing that your main focus and driving force should be your goals. If your goals are firm in your mind, your mind will seek ways to deal with obstacles."

"And," he continued, "obstacles indeed may be helpful in a number of ways... They may help you reaffirm – or disaffirm – your commitment to your goals... They may present challenges that cause you to pursue educational opportunities or other personal growth experiences... They may cause you to seek the help of others who can provide the assistance you need... In actuality, obstacles may help propel you towards your goals, rather than detract you from them. How you view the challenges you face, therefore, is extremely important to your ultimate success in achieving your goals."

Acton then looked directly at me. I readied myself for his magic. "My friend here," he said, nodding in my direction, "thinks I like playing with words!... Well, I do! That is because sometimes 'playing with words' can be helpful because, as a result, you may come across a different, more useful way of looking at things."

He looked at me again. "What is an obstacle?" he asked me.

"It's something that blocks your path," I replied.

Dr. Acton turned toward the blackboard and drew the shape of a cube, which he then filled in to look solid. Then, both in front and behind the cube, he drew what one could interpret as parts of a path – a common path.

"Something like this?" he asked me.

"Yes, I guess," I replied.

"Does anyone else have any thoughts about what an obstacle is?" the teacher asked the class.

"It is something that stops you," Kim suggested.

Dr. Acton extended the path a bit and then drew a 'stop' sign in its way. "Something like this?" he asked Kim.

"I guess you could depict it that way," Kim replied.

"It could be something that pulls you back," Joe volunteered.

Dr. Acton drew an outline figure of a man standing on the path in front of the solid block. He then drew outline figures of two other men who were grabbing the man and pulling him back towards the direction from which he had come.

"Something like this?" he asked Joe.

"Yes, something like that!" Joe replied.

Dr. Acton could draw pretty well. "Is there a 'Webster' in the class?" he asked.

No one in the class was named 'Webster', but Kelly apparently understood his hint. "I have 'Webster's New World Dictionary'!" she exclaimed.

"How does it define 'obstacle'?" Dr. Acton asked.

"It says it is 'anything that gets in the way or hinders; impediment; obstruction; hindrance" she replied. "'Obstacle is used of anything which literally or figuratively stands in the way of one's progress.'"

"Thank you, young woman... So, our definitions and depictions of what an obstacle is are fairly accurate. Would you agree, class?"

"Yes," we answered.

"So, who can define the word 'obfuscation'?" he then asked.

No hands were raised.

"Young woman," he asked Kelly, "Do you think perhaps 'Webster' could help us again?"

"Well," she replied, quickly turning the page for the answer. "It says 'to obfuscate' is 'to cloud over; obscure; make dark or unclear.' A second definition is 'to muddle; to confuse; bewilder.' The word 'obfuscation' is the noun form."

"So," Dr. Acton concluded, "We can consider 'obfuscations' to be things that cloud over, make unclear, or confuse..."

He walked to the blackboard at the back of the room and began drawing a path similar to the one he had drawn on the other blackboard. He again drew the outline figure of the man. But instead of drawing a big, solid cube in the path, he drew huge, dark clouds over the path, with rain pouring down at spots along the way. The old man drew various-sized puddles, too. And he wrote the words "MIXTURES OF DARKNESS AND BRIGHTNESS" over the horizon leading toward the "GOAL".

But that was not all. He also drew another path – in fact, two other paths – directly in front of the man, as well as more alternate paths further along the way. And, instead of having the other outline figures of men grabbing him and pulling him back, Acton drew two men who looked to be conferring with the goal-seeker.

Dr. Acton stepped back from the blackboard and glanced at his artwork. He then looked again at the front blackboard. The wise man apparently wasn't quite satisfied yet. He walked back to the blackboard and scribbled three words of graffiti on the path in front of the man: "THINK and GROW".

"Notice any differences in the drawings on the blackboards?" he asked us.

"Yes!" we answered.

"This drawing," John said, pointing to the rear blackboard, "seems to offer the man more hope toward reaching his goal."

"Why is that?" Dr. Acton asked.

"Because," John explained, "although it shows that the path is less clear, there are no insurmountable obstacles that make the path impassable. In the other drawing, it seems like the path is impassable."

"Would everyone agree with John?" Dr. Acton asked us.

Heads nodded in agreement. No one offered to disagree.

"John," the teacher continued, "Which drawing shows obstacles as roadblocks, and which shows them as obfuscations?"

"I think the drawing on the front blackboard shows them as roadblocks, and the one on the rear blackboard shows them as obfuscations," John replied.

"Do you agree, Class?" Dr. Acton asked.

The drawings were pretty clear. We nodded in agreement. Dr. Acton confirmed that we viewed his artwork as he had intended.

"My friends," the wise man preached, "YOU choose the path you take towards your goals. YOU choose whether to view challenges as obstacles or as obfuscations. YOU choose how you are going to respond to the mental images you confront when facing challenges. YOU choose whether you are going to let things or people stand in your way... The path to your goals may not be as clear as you would like or as easy to travel as you would prefer, but it does not have to be impassable."

He pointed to the 'graffiti' he had written. "I suggest you 'THINK and GROW' your way," he urged.

The old man began erasing the board, and we awaited our recap:

(59) Visualization can help you stay focused on your goals and may also help you see another path to reaching them.

(60) Perceptions and visualizations can help you overcome obstacles.

(61) It is difficult for some people to visualize their goals clearly without seeing roadblocks.

(62) If you have difficulty with your visualizations, practice them, concentrating on your goal and on eliminating any obstacles that may present themselves.

(63) If your goals are firm in your mind, your mind will seek ways to deal with obstacles.

(64) Obstacles may be helpful.

(65) Obstacles may help you reaffirm – or disaffirm – your commitment to your goals.

(66) Obstacles may present challenges that cause you to pursue educational opportunities or other personal growth experiences.

(67) Obstacles may cause you to seek the help of others who can provide the assistance you need.

(68) Obstacles may help propel you towards your goals, rather than detract you from them.

(69) How you view the challenges you face is extremely important to your ultimate success in achieving your goals.

Running out of room on the board, Dr. Acton walked to the blackboard at the front of the room. He erased it and continued:

(70) An obstacle is something that blocks your path, stops you, or pulls you back – anything which stands in the way of your progress.

(71) Obfuscations are things that cloud over, make unclear, or confuse.

(72) Thinking of challenges as obfuscations instead of as obstacles may make the path to one's goals seem more passable.

(73) YOU choose whether to view challenges as obstacles or as obfuscations.

(74) YOU choose the path you take toward your goals.

(75) YOU choose how you are going to respond to the mental images you confront when facing challenges.

(76) YOU choose whether you are going to let things or people stand in your way.

(77) The path to your goals may not be as clear as you would like or as easy to travel as you would prefer, but it does not have to be impassable.

(78) THINK and GROW your way to your goals.

Apparently satisfied he had presented enough noteworthy material for one evening, Dr. Acton suggested we take a few moments to contemplate what we had discussed.

As the old man turned to grab his portfolio, my classmates and I readied ourselves to grab our pens. Per his custom, Acton quickly strode out of the room. Per our custom, we began writing once again.

Most of us stayed for awhile, but it was interesting to see that Cathy and Mike were the first students to leave. Guess they decided to share the note-taking duties!

Neal R. Voron

Chapter 12

Dr. Acton probably didn't realize he not only helped Cathy and Mike get together, but he also drummed up some business for the local ice cream parlor!

While we eagerly awaited word about whether Cathy and Mike's date was successful, Sue announced that, after being inspired by those two, she had summoned the courage to ask Tom out for milkshakes, too. Tom had accepted, they had a good time, and now she couldn't wait to tell Dr. Acton!

The old man was almost literally knocked off his feet as Sue rushed toward him as he entered the room. Acton seemed genuinely and pleasantly surprised by his unexpected success.

"I sure am glad that Cathy and Tom like milkshakes!" he exclaimed, as he hoisted his portfolio onto the desk. "I guess things went well?" he asked in the direction of Cathy and Mike.

"We're going again tonight after class!" Cathy exclaimed.

"So are we!" Sue joined in, half-jumping out of her seat.

Mike and Tom were all smiles.

"I am happy for all of you!" Dr. Acton told them. "Does anyone else like milkshakes?"

"Why, thank you, Dr. Acton!" came a swift reply from Jim. "I thought you would never ask! Now, that wasn't too hard to do, was it?"

The class roared in laughter. Dr. Acton glanced at Jim and just smiled for a moment. Jim soaked in the attention.

"I am sorry, Jim," Dr. Acton told him. "I hope this rejection does not crush you, but I believe you misinterpreted my question. I was not offering you a milkshake."

"I know, Dr. Acton!" Jim replied with a smile. Then, extending his hand, he asked, "Can we just shake?"

The class roared again. Jim was funny and we knew Dr. Acton had a sense of humor, but how much 'flip' would the old man take?

Instead of shaking Jim's hand, Dr. Acton said, "Okay!" and began dancing by himself. "How does the song go?" he asked us. "Shake, baby, shake?"

The class roared again. Things were getting hysterical, but all of us – including Dr. Acton – were having fun.

The teacher stopped his brief dance and then actually walked over to Jim and shook his hand.

"Okay!" Dr. Acton said, as he returned to the front of the room, "Let us get started!"

The old man's eyes scanned the room. All 35 of us were present.

"Do you have your homework tonight?" he asked.

"Homework?" I thought, suddenly feeling panicked. A sense of unease filled the room.

"We didn't have homework, did we?" asked John.

"Of course you had homework!" Dr. Acton replied. "You always have homework!"

The teacher certainly had the class confused. Bill raised his hand.

"Dr. Acton, I don't remember being assigned any homework for tonight," he said.

"That is because I did not announce that I was assigning any!" Dr. Acton replied.

Now we were really confused!

"Students seeking to learn always have homework!" Acton explained. "You carry your lessons with you – up here," he said, pointing to his temple. "After you leave the classroom, your mind processes the information to which it has been exposed. You internalize and file it for future reference. Then, hopefully, when the information can be useful to you, you use it. Utilization of what you have been taught so that it benefits you and your personal goals is what makes your acquisition of knowledge worthwhile."

"So, you weren't expecting us to turn anything in to you?" John asked.

"No!" the teacher replied. "I can only handle so many 'obstacles' of yours at once. You have all committed enough to paper to satisfy me. I am more interested in what is going on in your heads with the concepts we have discussed during this course."

He paused for a moment and then startled us with his next comment.

"Actually, John," Dr. Acton continued, "all but a couple of you have your previous homework assignment here with you tonight – all except for Jim and Mike."

"Dr. Acton, what do you mean?" asked John. "You tore up the papers with our 'obstacles' that we submitted last class!"

"Yes, my friend, I did," the wise man said, "But unless you deal with those obstacles – as Jim and Mike did – or unless they mysteriously, miraculously disappear on their own, you still carry them with you! You see?"

The old man sure had an odd way of getting his point across, but he was successful.

"Now, I hope you were not too shocked when I discarded your homework assignments at our last class," Acton continued.

"As you are aware, I did read them," he explained, "And I now have an understanding of what each of you perceive your obstacle – or should I say obfuscation? – to be. Tonight we will look at them in general terms so we can understand the types of challenges that confront people."

"Most of the challenges the Class mentioned fall into one of several types," Dr. Acton said, walking toward the blackboard.

"One type of challenge involves confronting fear," he said, drawing a path cut-off by a huge cubed block on which he wrote the word "FEAR" in large letters.

"Here are some other types of challenges I gleaned from your homework assignments," he offered. He turned to the blackboard and drew four other separate paths that were blocked by huge cubed blocks.

On one block, the teacher wrote the words "SELF-IMPOSED LIMITATIONS".

On another block, Acton wrote "EXTERNALLY-IMPOSED LIMITATIONS".

On another, he wrote "LACK OF CONFIDENCE".

And, on yet another, he wrote "LACK OF RESOURCES".

Turning back to address us, Dr. Acton said, "Please understand that these are general categories for types of challenges based upon the 'obstacles' you gave me. There may be a general category or two that we missed, but these should cover most types."

He studied the board for a moment, and then wrote the words "Lack of Goals or Direction" in front of the block labeled "SELF-IMPOSED LIMITATIONS".

"Of course," he continued, "if you do not have an idea of what your goals are, it is difficult to determine the correct path to attain them. Would you agree?"

Heads nodded in agreement.

Kelly raised her hand. "Dr. Acton, before you continue, how do we determine what our goals are?"

"Good question, young woman!" the teacher replied. "Does anyone have any thoughts about how we determine what our goals are?"

"We think about what interests us," I offered.

"That sounds good," Dr. Acton replied.

"We determine what we need to do to be able to achieve whatever interests us. Those things are our goals, too," Nancy added.

"Anything else?" Dr. Acton asked.

"We prioritize which interests are most important to us so we can determine where to direct our efforts," suggested John.

"Well!" Dr. Acton exclaimed, "We have gone from determining what our goals are to determining how to pursue them. But your answers have been very good! In fact, it is important to determine what we need to do to achieve our goals so we can determine whether we still wish to pursue them! Some people, after learning what is necessary to achieve a particular goal, simply decide either the goal is not really important enough to them to merit the effort involved or that they are unwilling or unable to do what is necessary. So, they give up on their goal."

"And, as John mentioned," Dr. Acton continued, "Prioritizing our interests can help us determine where to direct our efforts to achieve our goals. There often are short-term or near-term steps that must be climbed before you are able to achieve your ultimate goal."

"Can you give us an example, Dr. Acton?" Mike asked.

"Certainly!" the wise man replied. "Let us say a fellow named Sam has a strong interest in being his own boss. That, he says, is his goal. However, Sam is not really sure what type of business he would like to pursue. Not only that, but he does not have money right now to invest in a business and he needs to earn money to pay for his household expenses. So, Class, what would you say is Sam's top priority?"

Several students called out "being his own boss," but many more said "earn money."

Cathy raised her hand, and began speaking. "I think doing something to earn money is the top priority because it is something Sam needs to do. Being his own boss can wait because Sam doesn't really need that – he wants it. Needs take priority over wants," she said.

"All of the time?" Dr. Acton asked her.

"In practice, no," Cathy replied. "But I think they should."

"Did you ever need a candy bar when you were little?" Dr. Acton asked. "Would you have been satisfied if your mother told you, 'No. You don't need it'?"

"Well," Cathy replied, "probably not. But, Dr. Acton, getting what you want is not always what is best for you."

"Would it have been okay for you to have gotten a candy bar as a treat after you had eaten dinner?" the teacher asked.

"Perhaps," Cathy answered.

"Would it have been okay two weeks later?" Dr. Acton asked.

"Perhaps, but I probably wouldn't have been happy having to wait," Cathy conceded.

"I see," Acton replied. "Now, if you had not eaten in a long time and were not likely to be near a food source for awhile, would your mother have been likely to be more agreeable to giving you the candy bar right away if she had one?"

"Absolutely!" Cathy answered. "But then eating the candy bar would have been more of a need than a want."

"So, everything is relative, depending upon the situation – and priorities can change – would you agree, Class?" the teacher asked.

We nodded in agreement.

"Getting back to our friend Sam, then," Acton continued. "Cathy's plan of action seems practical. We just need to keep in mind that it is how Sam perceives his own situation that counts. He is the one who assigns value and priority."

"So, let us assume that Sam follows Cathy's suggested action plan," Dr. Acton continued. "Because earning money is a goal that he assigns some priority, Sam decides to get a job working for someone else. 'Being his own boss' is still a goal, but he decides to make it a longer term goal."

"In the meantime, he can research different kinds of businesses he may wish to pursue," Acton noted. "He may start saving money to invest in his business, or he may seek to meet potential investors. Any one, or several, of those things could be actions associated with shorter term goals – such as obtaining financing – that will help Sam ultimately achieve his long term goal of being his own boss. Of course, Sam may someday change his mind and decide that is no longer a goal of his or that he is unwilling to put forth the effort to achieve it."

"So, Dr. Acton," Mike asked, "Are you saying that 'lack of focus,' 'lack of resources,' or 'delay' can be obstacles to achieving one's goals?"

"Yes, if one lets them be, son," the wise teacher replied. "Or, they could be 'obfuscations', muddying the road – perhaps prolonging the time it takes to achieve something – but not prohibiting achievement."

Dr. Acton walked to the blackboard. He added a slash and the word "Focus" next to the words "Lack of Goals or Direction" in front of the block labeled "SELF-IMPOSED LIMITATIONS."

He wrote the word "Money" in front of the block labeled "LACK OF RESOURCES."

Then he wrote the word "Delay" in front of two of the blocks: those labeled "SELF-IMPOSED LIMITATIONS" and "EXTERNALLY-IMPOSED LIMITATIONS."

"Both?" Mike asked, as the old man finished writing in front of the second block.

"Sure!" Dr. Acton replied. "You can delay yourself, or external influences can delay you. Sometimes, even the most well-tuned car gets a flat tire."

The old man walked to the back of the room and began writing on the blackboard:

(79) You carry your lessons with you in your mind.

(80) Utilization of what you have been taught so that it benefits you makes your acquisition of knowledge worthwhile.

(81) Unless you deal with your obstacles – or unless they mysteriously disappear on their own – you still carry them with you.

(82) If you do not have an idea of what your goals are, it is difficult to determine the correct path to attain them.

(83) To help determine your goals, think about what interests you and think about what you will need to do to achieve whatever those interests are.

(84) Some people are unwilling or unable to do what is necessary to achieve their goals.

(85) Prioritizing your interests can help you determine where to direct your efforts to achieve your goals.

(86) Remember, priorities can change.

(87) Consider wants versus needs. Which takes priority for you?

(88) Are your challenges self-imposed? Perhaps you can unimpose them.

Dr. Acton then put down the chalk and returned to the desk to grab his portfolio. We were surprised that he seemed ready to leave.

"I invite all of you," he suggested, "to sit for a few moments to consider your goals and the types of challenges you face. Think about what category or categories your challenges fall under. Then think about whether how you categorize your challenges impacts upon your perception of them."

"For example," he continued, "Perhaps you will realize that a particular challenge is self-imposed. If you find that to be the case, maybe you will also find a way to unimpose it upon yourself. Or, maybe you will realize that external factors impact upon you, and you can think about whether you can influence those factors in any way… Remember, my friends, I am just a facilitator – someone to help you to understand, to think, to see possibilities. YOU have to do the work. YOU have to see for yourselves where you stand... Think about it."

The blackboards loomed large as the elderly figure sprinted out of the room.

Neal R. Voron

Chapter 13

When Dr. Acton entered the room for our next class, he didn't bother to part with his portfolio. In fact, he seemed preoccupied, as if in a hurry to go somewhere.

"Is everyone here?" he asked, quickly counting heads as he scanned the room.

We were all present.

"Okay, I have a surprise!" Dr. Acton announced. "We are going on a field trip! Please gather your belongings and follow me."

That said, he started toward the door!

"A field trip now?" John asked.

"We'd better go," Nancy suggested, "or Dr. Acton will disappear, and we'll spend the whole night trying to find him!"

Everyone jumped from their seats and ran in pursuit of the old man. He was at the door as we entered the hallway. We followed him out of the building.

Parked right outside was a blue bus that looked like a school bus, except it said "Police Department" on its side.

"Everyone aboard!" Dr. Acton instructed.

We were surprised and intrigued.

"A police bus?" exclaimed Jim, as he boarded. "Why a police bus?"

"Would you believe it is because I wanted a captive audience, Jim?" the teacher asked.

"Again, Dr. Acton?" Jim replied. "You had us captive before when the classroom door was jammed shut... Wow! Look at these seats!"

We quickly noticed that the seats in the bus were specially-equipped with devices that apparently could be used to shackle prisoners being transported.

"Dr. Acton, I haven't been that bad, have I?" Jim asked.

"Not that bad," the fatherly figure reassured him.

"Please be seated," Dr. Acton urged us. "We do not have far to travel. And do not worry... you are not being taken to jail! We have been invited to be guests for a tour of the Police Development Training Center by Sgt. Elmore Ready, a training specialist there, who I have known for some time. He generously arranged for our transportation. Sgt. Ready will give us some insights into how he prepares police officers for the challenges they face. Please be attentive so you can learn as much as possible. Sgt. Ready is a good person from whom to learn."

Dr. Acton did not need to ask for our attention. We were revved up already.

Upon arrival at our destination, we were greeted by Sergeant Ready, a huge, but well-proportioned, man with a stern, military-like appearance.

"It's good to see you again, Dr. Acton," he said, offering the old man a firm handshake. His voice was loud and sounded authoritative. "Is this our new group of potential achievers?" he asked, glancing toward our group with a half-smile.

"My friend, Sgt. Ready, it is good to see you, too," Dr. Acton replied. "We appreciate your taking time from your busy schedule to help us on our journey on 'The Obstacle Course.' Not only do we have potential achievers, Sergeant, we have potential believers."

"Believers? Dr. Acton, you actually brought some people who think they can succeed against 'The Obstacle Course'?" Sgt. Ready asked.

"Well, I do not really know if they believe they can succeed, but I believe they can," Acton declared.

It felt good to hear Dr. Acton express his confidence in our class. Instantly, 35 students became believers that they could be achievers. "We won't let him down!" I thought.

Turning towards us, Sgt. Ready announced, "Welcome to the Police Development Training Center. This is where the finest area police officer candidates are trained to serve and to protect our families and our communities. Dr. Acton has requested that I provide you with a tour of our facility, so if you will follow me, we will begin."

We followed Sgt. Ready and Dr. Acton down a hallway that was lined with hundreds of plaques on each side. Consecutive rows of names of graduating officers were accented only by the conspicuous appearance of an occasional black ribbon. A large sign proclaimed, "We opened our minds and hearts to serve and to protect..."

Sgt. Ready led us into a room that resembled a small chapel and asked that we be seated. Upon entering, he removed his hat, revealing a huge scar at the top of his forehead on his left side. The room featured another wall with plaques and portraits – these honoring the memory of three officers who had fallen in the line of duty. The inscription above the plaques read, "We opened our minds and hearts to serve and to protect… and so we did, so others may live."

The bright and friendly faces adorning the portraits belied their tragic fates. We sat quietly for a moment and, following Sgt. Ready's lead, bowed our heads in silence.

"If my worst fate should be that I die so that others may live," the police veteran declared, "Then I would say that the goal was worth the effort. Fear motivates me to train and prepare myself for anything that may happen, but it does not stop me from doing my job. My fallen friends – and, indeed, I knew each of these three officers very well – they gave their best and they made a difference in the lives of many people… a big difference."

Sgt. Ready paused again to reflect for a moment and then asked us to follow him. He led us to another room that was similar to our classroom at school. He stood at the front of the room as we sat down. Dr. Acton, portfolio in hand, sat down, too – between John and Bill.

"I know you didn't come here just to sit in a classroom," Sgt. Ready said. "But we are going to stay here for a few minutes so I can acquaint you with some important information."

He continued, "This Center is entrusted with a huge responsibility of preparing police officers to provide quality law enforcement services. An integral component of that training is to ensure that officers are mentally and physically ready for the duties of their job and for the many, often spontaneous, situations and challenges they will encounter."

"All officer candidates are introduced to the Center in the exact manner in which you were. We bring them here for the first time on the bus to familiarize them with the bus itself. As I am sure you noticed, the bus is equipped with special restraints for the transport of prisoners. We also use the bus for transportation of officers in situations where we need a large police force presence. It is our belief that firsthand exposure to our equipment and capabilities increases officers' knowledge and understanding and decreases their levels of uncertainty or apprehension. We don't want any unnecessary or undue influences to block or hinder an officer's performance; there are plenty of variables already over which we have no control, so we try to control as many as we can."

Sgt. Ready then continued explaining their method of introducing officer candidates to the Center. "We walk the candidates along the hall honoring our graduates to acquaint them with the level of respect we show towards our goals as officers and towards those who have achieved degrees of success in attaining those goals. Hopefully, the plaques on the wall also serve as motivating forces for them."

"Then, we visit the memorial chapel to pay tribute to our fallen brethren and contemplate the reality of the path we have chosen to pursue. If any candidates, at that point, experience a change of heart regarding their pursuit of a police career, they are entitled to return transportation and our thanks for considering police service. This type of career is not for everyone. Some people are unwilling to expose themselves to certain risks in pursuit of their goals. Therefore, they sometimes must modify their goals. For the Police Department, some of the occupational risks are unavoidable. We really don't want officers who are unwilling to accept the risks. They would have great difficulty doing their jobs well and could possibly put themselves, fellow officers, and the public in danger."

"So," he continued, "What we do is bring the remaining candidates in here and begin the process of preparing them to be the best possible police officers, ready to deal with challenges that come their way, so they can achieve their goals successfully and with minimal risk to their personal well-being."

Sgt. Ready paused for a moment. Dr. Acton took advantage of the opportunity to ask a question.

"Sgt. Ready," he asked, "Are you saying that people should acknowledge their self-imposed limitations and then modify their goals, if necessary?"

"Yes," the sergeant replied. "Either do that or get rid of their self-imposed limitations – and I mean get totally rid of them. Doing the latter can be extremely difficult, if not impossible, for some people. That's why we think police officer candidates who cannot accept the risks involved with police work should not pursue police work. We cannot have a police force comprised of people who are unwilling to enter dangerous situations."

Dr. Acton followed with another question. "A candidate's self-awareness and attitude, then, are important factors in becoming a successful police officer?"

"Yes. Absolutely," Sgt. Ready replied. "At our center, we spend a lot of time stressing the importance of one's attitude towards police work. We also do extensive classroom training on all aspects of policing. But, enough for now about classroom training! This is a field trip for you! Let's continue our tour."

Sgt. Ready motioned for Dr. Acton and the class to follow him out of the room and down the hall. He had us peer through windows to see trainees taking shooting practice at both mobile and stationary targets. Down another hallway were several exercise rooms filled with mats, weights, bikes, and all sorts of high-tech machinery. We saw a classroom that was specially designed for first-aid and health issues training.

In the halls and classrooms, many signs with educational or motivational messages were posted. Among them were: "TOUGH doesn't have to mean ROUGH", "Innocent until proven guilty – it's the law!", "YOU can make a difference", "One never KNOWS exactly what will happen – BE PREPARED"...

That last one really caught my attention. It sounded so familiar!

Sgt. Ready showed us the Center's dining hall, which offered fresh salads, real fruit juices, and other healthy items, but, he assured us, no doughnuts! That comment elicited a few laughs. Jim, thankfully, did not act obnoxious.

It was interesting to note that the Center also had several of what Sgt. Ready called "stress management suites and group rooms" that were regularly staffed by professional psychotherapists. "All of our officer candidates are required to be in therapy," he informed us. "We want to ensure their mental, as well as physical, health."

He then took us to the Center's gym. It was deceptively gigantic and unlike any we had ever seen before. Upon first entering the gym, it looked incredibly small: all one could see was a computer, a desk, a chair, and another door! Sgt. Ready explained that the gym was set-up to challenge candidates both mentally and physically. The computer presented them with personalized interactive mental challenges on its video screen, and upon completion of the computer test, the candidates could enter the main area of the gym for the physical challenges, which were presented in the form of a large obstacle course and simulated firearm confrontation. Ready took us through a special entrance to a second floor balcony so we could view the entire gym.

What a sight! It was the ultimate obstacle course, complete with blockades, mazes, tires, enclosures, illusory effects, ground impediments, tunnels, walls, chain ladders, hurdles, ropes, rings, trampolines, peg boards, pools of water, varied lighting levels, and many physically challenging obstacles – some of which were set-up to be activated upon one's approach to them. The firearm challenge was the last part of the course. I wondered why, and apparently, so did others.

"Sgt. Ready, why is the 'firearm skills challenge' the last part of the course?" Nancy asked.

"Good question!" Dr. Acton called out to Nancy.

"Well, the answer is simple," Sgt. Ready replied. "If a police officer candidate is not ready for a firearm confrontation at any moment – including when he or she is tired after running, climbing, swimming, or jumping – then the candidate is not ready to be a police officer. We're tough here because it's a tough world out there. We don't do anybody a favor if we don't produce the best-prepared police officers."

Dr. Acton indicated to Sgt. Ready that it was nearing time for us to return to school. He thanked him for the tour on behalf of the class.

"It was my pleasure," Sgt. Ready told us. "I hope your trip here has provided you with some insight that can help you in dealing with your own individual goals. I would like to share just one more personal observation with you before you leave... It has been my experience that those candidates who enter our training center with a genuine interest 'to serve and to protect'... with an attitude, a belief, that they can 'make a difference'... with a clear understanding of the reality of the path they are pursuing... with an open mind to learning... and with a willingness, a dedication, to being prepared and doing 'what it takes' to be successful – those are the candidates who are successful here and in their lives. I wish you all the best."

Sgt. Ready led us back to the bus, and it wasn't long before we were on our way back to school.

"I think I want to be a police officer," Jim told Dr. Acton.

"Is that so?" the old man replied. "Then, go for it, my friend! If that's what you want, then go for it! You certainly have an idea about what will be involved."

Somehow, I had trouble picturing Jim as a police officer. But if he could pass Sgt. Ready's training program, I would certainly be impressed, as would the rest of our class.

We arrived back at school, with John commenting that was the last time he ever wanted to ride on a police bus.

Dr. Acton, portfolio in hand, told us there was no need to return to the classroom this evening. "Just one thing," he told us, "Next class is 'Play Day'. Be prepared! See you!"

"Play Day?" we thought. "Be prepared? What did he want us to do?"

Before we could ask, old man Acton had sprinted down the street and turned the corner. Gone again, as usual! We would just have to wait and see.

Neal R. Voron

Chapter 14

Dr. Acton apparently was serious about "Play Day." He entered the room pulling a hand truck, upon which was a large box and his tattered portfolio.

We were curious. What was in the box?

Dr. Acton asked us to move our desk chairs towards the walls of the room in order to create a large space on the floor in the center of the room.

He reached into the box and pulled out four large, square oil cloths, which he placed on the floor.

"Okay, don't just sit there! Gather around!" the teacher instructed.

As we took seats on the floor, he pulled out packages of fresh clay, crayons, construction paper, scissors, paste, pipe cleaners, wooden sticks and building blocks.

"Grab whatever supplies interest you!" Dr. Acton urged. "There are plenty to go around! Today is 'Play Day.' It is time to have FUN!"

We reached out like eager little kids who were getting presents from their grandfather.

"What do you want us to do, Dr. Acton?" asked John.

"I simply want you to think about this course and create something, whatever it may be," our leader replied. "Go ahead!" he said, clapping his hands to get our attention. "Get started!"

A murmur of voices pierced the hesitation, and 35 class members began to play – some spending time quietly contemplating a plan of action, while others immediately plunged into action.

I paused for a moment, unsure of what I wanted to do. Then I reached for a square of clay and began to knead it. The hard, cool gray earthen substance quickly became soft and warm in my hands. Dr. Acton stood over my shoulder for a moment.

"Clay is quite malleable, my friend. Would you agree?" he asked.

There was that word again – malleable. My mind quickly searched for its meaning. When did he use that word before?... Oh, I remembered: "Self-imposed limitations are malleable. That means you can change them."

I looked up at Dr. Acton. "Yes, the clay is quite malleable, Doctor," I replied, as I started rolling the mass between my palms. "I could probably mold it into anything I wanted – if I could only think of what to create!"

"Yes, I am sure you probably could," he said. "You have changed a cube into a sphere already! Keep at it!"

The wise man walked away, and I glanced downward to see that I had indeed molded a sphere. "What should I do?" I thought. "What should I do?"

I glanced around to peek at what others were doing. Kim had grabbed some blocks and was using clay as a type of mortar to join them together. Nancy was busy cutting several different-colored sheets of construction paper simultaneously into what looked like confetti. Joe was pasting some sticks together. And John was shaping some red clay into snake-like shapes.

I decided to shape the clay into a runner who would be leaning forward – like someone running on a track or an obstacle course. As I kept my mind focused on my inner vision of what the runner would look like, my fingers determinedly formed the clay into the desired shape. I wasn't worried about fine details, like facial features or clothes. The form was what mattered to me, and I was pretty happy with what I had created through my efforts. The clay had made it easy to smooth over or reshape whatever I did not like, and I realized that I was the only judge whose opinion would count in my book.

After I finished the runner, I took some sticks and cut and pasted them to create a few hurdles for the runner to leap over. I grabbed some red clay to mold into supports for the hurdles. Then I positioned the runner in front of the hurdles, as if ready to confront them.

I stared for a minute at what I had created and decided I was done. The masterpiece was complete.

Dr. Acton walked by again and tapped my shoulder. "Are the hurdles obstacles or obfuscations?" he asked. "Do not tell me. Just think about it."

I looked up at him and just smiled. He smiled back and walked away.

The old man seemingly could make anything relevant to his teachings.

I thought about Dr. Acton's question and determined that the hurdles could be either, depending upon how one wanted to look at them.

I watched in amazement as my classmates threw their energies full blast into their artwork. Each person, in his or her own way, was remarkably creative!

Kim had built a wall of blocks with a hole in the middle and clay snake-like figures climbing around, through and over it.

Nancy had molded a clay figure of a man who was surrounded by multi-colored confetti but still reaching forward with his hands toward a sign marked "GOAL."

Joe had built steps which led from the ground over some blocks and mounds of clay to what a crayoned sign called "The Next Level."

John had flattened his clay to create what looked like a network of pathways, and he positioned a pipe cleaner stick figure at a crossroads.

Seeing these creations, I wondered what Jim had done. I looked to the back of the room and noticed that he had secluded himself in the corner with some paper and crayons. He was seated on a desk chair and kept looking up at Dr. Acton, who was over-seeing my classmates' activities. Whenever the teacher glanced his way, Jim would position his hands to cover his artwork and motion to Dr. Acton to stay away. The old man obliged.

Eventually, Dr. Acton urged everyone to finish with their work, and a few minutes later he called for our attention.

"Did you have FUN?" he asked.

"Yes!" came the replies.

"This was really different!" Nancy said.

"Nancy, every class here is different!" John remarked.

"Well, was the difference helpful?" Dr. Acton asked.

"Yes," Nancy replied, as many of us nodded in agreement. "It presented us with a way to get in touch with our feelings and with our creativity. I realized I feel more upbeat about my abilities and potential than I did before I took this course."

"That is terrific, Nancy!" Dr. Acton replied. "I hope 'Play Day' was helpful to all of you. I have learned that play manifests some wonderfully healthful, restorative, creative energy that too many people do not realize they have and that too few do not utilize nearly often enough to derive the benefits it offers."

"What do you think of what we created, Dr. Acton?" John asked.

"I think all of your artistic expressions are important reflections of who you are and how you view things. Other than that, John, I do not judge your artwork," the wise man replied. "I think all of you are wonderfully talented individuals, with many different abilities, with remarkable creativity, and with fantastic potential to reach within yourselves to achieve whatever it is you seek."

"Are there any specific things, other than what you have already mentioned, Dr. Acton, that you think we should learn from 'Play Day'?" John asked.

"I am glad you asked that, John," Dr. Acton replied. "I was going to suggest that you think about the thought process you went through to decide what you would create... Think about how your creation evolved – what changes occurred, and why... Think about whether you sought advice or encouragement from others, and why... Think about whether you judged the merit or the result of your artwork, and why... Think about how, having the same supplies available, everyone's creation was different in some way... Think about how, with crayons, you can use two colors to make a third color... Think about how, with clay, you can mold three-dimensional objects or figures with limited or fine detail – and you can modify or destroy those figures with relatively little effort..."

"Most importantly," he continued. "Think about how much FUN 'play' is... Think about the role of play in your life... Think about how play can help you to feel better, to express your creativity, to communicate, to learn, to understand, to see possibilities, and to grow into the person you wish to be."

The old man looked towards our artwork. "I also suggest you stay here for a few minutes to look at each other's work. Perhaps you will learn something by seeing how others approach things," he said.

He looked directly at me and, then, at my artwork. "You know, in 'The Obstacle Course,' hurdles are part of the course. The best hurdlers learn to take them in stride."

Wow! What an association! Week by week, I was growing more and more appreciative – and envious – of his wit.

Dr. Acton grabbed the scissors and paste and then started handing out the remaining clay and other supplies.

"'Play Day' does not have to be one day in a class, my friends," he said. "You can make 'Play Day' any day and every day."

Dr. Acton tossed the scissors, paste, and oil cloths into the box, then grabbed his portfolio and the hand truck. He asked us to be sure to pick-up our artwork and rearrange the chairs before we leave.

"Wait, Dr. Acton! Don't go!" yelled Jim, as the old man started wheeling the hand truck towards the door.

Dr. Acton was startled as he looked back at Jim. The entire class looked back at Jim.

"Please take just a moment to look at what I did!" Jim begged. "I wanted to show it to you... but after it was finished..."

He held up a large piece of beige construction paper, on which he had drawn an amazingly accurate portrait of Dr. Acton! It looked terrific! Our class had no idea Jim was such a wonderful artist.

Apparently, neither did Dr. Acton. His eyes swelled up with tears, and he was at a momentary loss for words.

"Jim, that is so nice!" he said. "It is so nice!"

Jim offered to give it to him, but Dr. Acton politely refused.

"Please keep it to help you remember what you have learned in this course," the teacher suggested.

The old man offered his thanks and suggested that perhaps Jim's artistic talent would be helpful to the police force, if Jim was truly interested in becoming an officer as he had said.

Then the old man left.

I stayed with my classmates and reviewed the work the others had done. It was all quite uplifting and energizing, except for Bill's, which made me feel sad. He had simply written the word "COURAGE" on a wooden block.

Chapter 15

Could our next class even come close to the excitement of our field trip and "Play Day"? As we awaited Dr. Acton's arrival, we hoped that something exciting would happen. In fact, we were probably looking too hard for something to happen.

When Dr. Acton entered the classroom at 7 p.m., it took no more than two seconds for Jim and friends in the back of the room to begin laughing hysterically. As Dr. Acton walked toward the desk, the whole class saw why: he looked particularly well-endowed this evening.

"Good evening!" Dr. Acton greeted us, with a smile. "It sounds like we are ready for some fun tonight, right Jim?"

"It looks that way, Dr. Acton!" Jim wisecracked. That remark elicited more laughs and more than a few muffled laughs.

Dr. Acton stood in front of us looking amused.

"Good, good!" he said. "Even though it is not 'Play Day,' there is no reason why this class cannot be fun!"

He reached into his front trouser pocket and produced his "endowment" – a rectangular prism. Instantly, the room seemed aglow with sunlight, as the geometric wonder seemed to draw the rays of the sun to it like a magnet. And, just as suddenly, a rainbow shined brightly on the ceiling.

"Would any of you have guessed that I was carrying a rainbow in my pocket?" the teacher asked.

"No, Dr. Acton, but knowing you, I'm not surprised!" Jim exclaimed. "I'm just surprised that it fit in your pocket!"

"Well, Jim, let me ask you – was it really there?" Dr. Acton asked.

"A rainbow? In your pocket?" Jim questioned in amazement.

"Yes. Was the rainbow in my pocket?" Acton repeated.

"No. The prism was in your pocket," Jim answered.

"Then where was the rainbow?" the teacher asked.

"It didn't exist," Jim replied.

"Are you sure, Jim?" Dr. Acton asked. "Class, does everyone agree with Jim?"

Most heads nodded in agreement, but Tom was outspoken in his disagreement. "Of course it existed," he said. "We just couldn't see it before! There are rainbows everywhere!"

"Very interesting comments, Tom. Can you explain?" Dr. Acton asked.

"The prism just helps us see light in a different way by refracting it to show a rainbow of the visible colors of the spectrum," Tom said. "The colors exist, but we need help – like from a prism – to see them in the form of a rainbow."

"So, Tom, if we brought a prism into a totally dark room, we would see a rainbow?" Dr. Acton asked.

"No. No, we wouldn't," Tom replied. "As I mentioned, a prism helps us see light in a different way. If there is no light, we won't be able to see a rainbow."

"Fascinating!" Dr. Acton exclaimed. "So, there is the potential to see rainbows anywhere there is light. But in places of total darkness, like inside my pocket, we could not see a rainbow. Would you agree, Tom?"

"Yes, I now agree," Tom replied.

The teacher rested his chin on his open palm. "I guess Jim was right! The rainbow was not in my pocket. Class, isn't it amazing how this simple tool – the prism – can make us see something we could not otherwise see?"

We nodded in agreement.

"Class, I brought the prism here today to help you see beyond the obvious," Dr. Acton said. "The real world we live in is constantly changing, and too often we become stuck both in our thinking and in how we approach change."

"How do we overcome the challenges we face?" he asked. "Each situation is unique, and each situation must be addressed based upon its unique circumstances. We can follow established guidelines, procedures, or recommendations, but it is important to remember that what has worked for someone else may not work for us. And, what has worked for us may not work for us again. So, if we create a specific plan of action for a particular challenge, we need to remain flexible to adjust it as necessary."

"By going forth with a plan, we face challenges proactively," Dr. Acton said. "Without a plan or by adjusting a plan when necessary, we face challenges reactively. It is important to be appropriately proactive and reactive to achieve the greatest success."

"If your challenge concerns a FEAR or LACK OF CONFIDENCE," he continued, "Proactive measures to combat it could possibly include building your self-esteem through preparation – that is: training and practice; positive thinking; making reasonable assumptions; and planning. Contingency planning – advance planning done in the event certain situations arise – is a proactive way to help assure a preferred reactive response. Reactive measures could include being open-minded and flexible enough to adapt to the conditions you face."

Cathy raised her hand to ask a question. "Dr. Acton, are you saying that we should simply ignore any fears that we have?" she asked. "It's not quite that easy!"

"Good question, young woman!" he replied. "Overcoming fear is not easy for many people. In fact, I often suggest that individuals having difficulties overcoming fear or a lack of confidence see a psychotherapist for professional help. I believe people can acknowledge their fears, yet see past them to prevent those fears from incapacitating them."

"What makes you think that?" asked John.

"The power of visualization, which we demonstrated earlier in this course," Dr. Acton replied. "It can be used to make things disappear in one's mind, and it can also be used to make things appear."

"Like fear?" asked Nancy.

"Like fear," Acton declared. "A father may be afraid of swimming, but, if his child is drowning and no help is available, he swims to save his child."

"But the fear may still be there," Nancy suggested.

"True, but, if the man swims to save his child, he learns that the fear is not strong enough to block him," the teacher replied.

"What if he doesn't swim to save his child?" Nancy asked.

"Then, my friend, he and his child are in trouble," Dr. Acton said. "Over the years, though, I think human nature generally favors the man seeing past his fear and swimming to save his child."

"Now," he continued, "When your goals seem blocked by a LACK OF RESOURCES, you could possibly look to acquire those resources on your own. You can also enlist the help of others who can provide the resources you need. For example, you enlisted my help in teaching you about dealing with obstacles by taking this course... speaking of which, it is time for some more notes."

The teacher turned to the blackboard and began to write:

(89) Play manifests healthful, restorative, creative energy.

(90) Play can help you to feel better, to express your creativity, to communicate, to learn, to understand, to see possibilities, and to grow into the person you wish to be.

(91) You can make "Play Day" any day and every day.

(92) We can see beyond the obvious if we seek to.

(93) The real world we live in is constantly changing. Too often we become stuck both in our thinking and in how we approach change.

(94) Each situation is unique and must be addressed based upon its unique circumstances. What worked before may not work again.

(95) By going forth with a plan, we face challenges proactively.

(96) Without a plan, or by adjusting a plan when necessary, we face challenges reactively.

(97) It is important to be appropriately proactive and reactive to achieve the greatest success.

Dr. Acton paused for a moment to review what he had written. He then turned towards us and said, "I hope you feel this course has been giving you a 'thinking framework' for successful personal growth and for progress towards your goals. And I hope it is helping to instill in each of you the confidence to use that framework. Your minds are very powerful tools you can use for your benefit. Obstacles do not have to block you from achieving your dreams."

Apparently the old man had taught enough for today. He grabbed his portfolio and readied himself to depart.

"Oh, before I forget," he said, stopping near the door. "We only have two more class meetings for this course. Next time, I will announce what you can look forward to for our last class!"

The old man gave us a wide smile and a wink. Then, before we knew it, he had left the room.

Chapter 16

We all arrived at class anxious to hear the "announcement" Dr. Acton said he would make regarding our last class meeting.

What could we look forward to this time? Dr. Acton always piqued our interest and kept us in suspense!

I must admit that, over a period of time, I was really coming to enjoy anticipating unknown events and then seeing and confronting them – regardless of whatever they happened to be and whenever they happened to occur.

Little did we know, though, what would occur in this class meeting, and we became concerned when 7:00 p.m. passed without Dr. Acton's arrival.

7:05 p.m. came and went... 7:10... 7:15... 7:20...

Everybody was still patiently waiting for Dr. Acton – even Jim and friends – but we were worried that he was this late.

"I'll go to the classroom next door," Jim volunteered. "I'll even check all the classrooms on this floor." John offered to inquire down at the administrative office. Mike said he would check at the faculty lounge. The three left the room together and started down the hall.

They found Dr. Acton almost immediately, as he was exiting – of all places – the bathroom! He did not look well. John and Mike ran over to aid him while Jim ran back to the classroom to ask Cathy, who's a nurse, for help.

"He's really sick!" Jim said. "He's as white as a ghost!"

Cathy ran down the hallway after urging everyone to stay calm and stay put so Dr. Acton wouldn't get unnecessarily alarmed.

After assessing the situation, Cathy suggested that John call for an ambulance. Dr. Acton, however, would not permit it.

"I am feeling better," he told them. "I can handle it. Let us get started with class!"

It wasn't too long before Dr. Acton slowly walked into the room, flanked by Cathy, Mike, and John.

"Good evening!" he said to the class, trying to jar himself into feeling better. "Sorry I am a bit late. I am afraid that something I ate did not quite agree with me! Thank you for your concern."

The old man motioned for Cathy, Mike, and John to sit down, and he, himself, sat down behind the desk after leaning his portfolio against its side. He did not look good.

"Now, let us get started!" Acton said while loosening his tie and unbuttoning his collar.

"It occurs to me," he said. "It occurs to me," he repeated, "That somehow I failed to mention to you earlier... I should have mentioned to you much earlier... something very important."

A bunch of us exchanged glances, wondering what he would say that was so important. I could still read concern about the teacher's health on many a brow.

"What I should have told you is that there are some things everyone should do to prepare to handle any challenges you may face… and they are: getting proper sleep, nutrition, and exercise. If you are not feeling fit and well, it is difficult to perform optimally," he said.

His point was painfully obvious. No wonder he thought to mention this now!

He started unbuttoning and rolling up his sleeves. His face was showing more color, but he was perspiring and he looked to be in considerable pain.

"Dr. Acton," Jim called out. "I think you're right. How about it if we make a deal? Let's stop class now so you can get some help and feel better, and we'll just stay longer for the last class. What do you say?"

You could tell by Jim's voice and manner that he was being sincere, not flippant as usual.

Cathy quickly voiced her approval of Jim's suggestion, and the entire class echoed the motion.

Jim stood up and walked to the blackboard. He wrote:

(98) Prepare to handle any challenges you may face: get proper sleep, nutrition, and exercise.

(99) If you are not feeling fit and well, it is difficult to perform optimally.

Jim paused a moment, stared at Dr. Acton, and then added one more note – totally on his own:

(100) What you feed your mind is as important as what you feed your body.

Acton probably couldn't believe his ears and his eyes. Was this the same Jim he had come to know?

"I appreciate your thoughts and your thoughtfulness, my friend," he told Jim. "That is a most important point you added, son. You must all feed yourself healthy, positive messages on a consistent basis. Always tell yourself that you CAN succeed! That is a major theme of this course."

We heard the old man's message, but Dr. Acton physically still looked like a desperate soul wanting to wage a battle he knew he could not win. Before he could reply to Jim's suggestion, Nancy stood up and proposed that everyone leave.

"Wait!" the old man begged. "Wait just a minute!"

Obediently, Nancy sat down. Acton momentarily rubbed his forearms as he contemplated what to do.

"Okay, we will do as Jim suggested," he said. "But let me just mention what I said I would announce today that you can look forward to for your last class."

We decided we could stay a moment longer to hear that.

"I plan to throw you a little party," he said, to our extreme surprise and delight. "So, make sure not to eat too much dinner before class... AND, if it is okay with you, I will invite my wife so she can meet the new graduates..."

"AND..." he smiled broadly, bringing more color into his face, "Remember I said early on that you would learn where you stand regarding grades? You will learn that next week, too! Okay?"

"Okay!" came the resounding reply.

To me, that sounded great. "Who wouldn't want a party? Who wouldn't want to meet Mrs. A.?" I thought. "But didn't he tell us before not to worry about grades? Why would he volunteer to discuss the topic? Well, I guess we'll find out!"

"Goodnight!" the teacher offered. "Thanks for being such caring people! You make me proud!"

Cathy, Mike, John, Nancy, and Bill all went to assist the old man on his way out of the room and the building. He grabbed his bag and walked slowly.

I was concerned. It was not his usual departure.

"Hope you feel better, soon!" I offered.

"Thanks, my friend. I will!" he replied.

I watched the group split up outside the building. Dr. Acton, who lived just over a block away from the school, insisted on going his own separate way.

Soon, he was gone.

Neal R. Voron

Chapter 17

It was 5 p.m., and I was contemplating whether to eat dinner at all because Dr. Acton's party was to be at 7 p.m.

It wound up being a good thing that I hadn't eaten.

The phone rang unexpectedly. It was some administrator from the school. He said he had an important message for me: the class meeting had to be canceled.

"Okay," I thought.

Then he said the class was not going to meet again.

"Huh, what?" I thought, surprised and alarmed.

"Why? What do you mean?" I asked.

"I am sorry to inform you that your class, 'The Obstacle Course', taught by Dr. Acton, will not be meeting again because... I regret to inform you... that... Dr. Acton has passed away."

"Passed away?" I thought. "You mean he died?" I asked him. I couldn't believe my ears!

"Yes, I regret to inform you... that he died," the caller said.

The old man died! My face started feeling hot and my heart felt like it had stopped beating.

"Hello?" came the voice on the phone. "Are you okay?"

"Uh, yes... uh, NO!" I told him.

"I am very sorry to have had to give you this news," the man said.

"I'm very sorry that you had to give me the news, too," I told him. "But thanks for letting me know. Do you know what happened to cause his death?"

"Only that he passed away gently in his sleep. Apparently, he was not feeling well lately," the man said.

"I feel so sad," I said, holding back tears.

"The school will make its counseling staff available, if you wish," he told me. He gave me the phone number, and I thanked him.

"Oh, two more things I must mention," he said. "The first thing is that you are welcome to attend a memorial service that will be held at the school on Thursday at 10:00 a.m. The second thing is that you will not be receiving a grade for the course."

I couldn't believe he felt he had to tell me that piece of information right then! I thanked him and quickly ended our conversation.

"Who cares about a grade for that class?" I thought. "I haven't cared about that for a long time!" The more I had thought about it, the grades didn't mean anything to me – learning the material taught was what mattered.

I didn't eat dinner at all that night. Instead, I sat alone in a darkened room with a lighted candle illuminating my mind to all the special qualities that Ernest Acton had possessed and had shared freely with me and my classmates. His fate did not seem fair because he had so much left to offer.

There was to be no party – just a memorial service. I did not know if I would ever have the opportunity to meet his wife. I would never know what Dr. Acton was going to tell us about our grades. We would not even get our last lesson or two.

The candle had not burned long when I deeply realized a great sense of loss.

There would be no more Dr. Acton – our great teacher and friend. We were, once again, on our own.

Neal R. Voron

Chapter 18

The excitement was gone, and the harsh realities of life were smacking us right in the face. "The fortunate few" gathered at the school for the memorial service.

We tried to console each other and boost our spirits. We would be okay, we told ourselves... After all, we had completed "The Obstacle Course." Or hadn't we?

There was heartfelt sadness as we mourned the loss of the mentor we had come to respect and to love. Each class we had shared with Dr. Acton had been a gift that had enriched us. Now, with the class over and him gone, we faced our uncertain futures with mixed emotions of feeling confident, yet poorer.

I counted 35 other familiar faces in attendance to honor Dr. Acton. Bill was there, looking like he was about to cry. Nancy was crying. John sought to console her. Jim was there, looking as white as a ghost. Sgt. Ready also paid his respects.

I didn't bother to count the other faces. The entire hall was filled with more of "the fortunate few" – lots more! It quickly became clear how fortunate we really were.

The ceremony was simple. At precisely 10:00 a.m., a sprightly old woman with a warm, built-in smile took a few quick strides to the podium and introduced herself to everyone as Dr. Sara Acton, our late friend's wife.

Before continuing to speak, she took a glance at the huge crowd and then to the stage at her side. There stood an empty chair next to a desk. Atop the desk was a familiar-looking old portfolio... Dr. Acton's.

"For the last 50 years, my friends," the old woman began, "I had not known a single day without my dear Ernie..."

"He brought me warmth and joy and love – qualities he shared with everyone he met. He was a special man, living his life the way he wanted, yet always considerate of others..."

"Ernie was unpredictable, but he made life exciting. He enjoyed 'challenges'. He was the smartest man I have ever known."

Then tears began to pour down her cheeks.

"I am going to miss him," she said. "I am not sure how I am going to cope..."

Tears flowed freely throughout the room.

"...But I will!" she declared.

"You will," I thought. "You will! I know you will!" Mrs. Acton seemed to be pretty special herself.

"I want to thank each and every one of you for joining with me to remember my husband," she continued. "He cared about all of you very much."

She then surprised everyone by asking Bill Telman to come forward. It was Bill from our class! Clearly, he was surprised, too, but he walked up to her side. He looked nervous.

"Bill," Mrs. Acton said, giving him a kiss and a hug, "On behalf of Dr. Acton and me, please accept, as a representative of all the students Ernie taught, this special memento..."

She walked to the desk and picked up the old portfolio! Then she handed it to Bill!

Tears came pouring from Bill's eyes... and he wasn't the only one with that problem. Bill gave her a kiss and hugged her.

"Bill, please keep it," Mrs. Acton instructed. "Ernie wanted you to have it."

Bill regained his composure and looked especially proud. The old man couldn't have chosen a better recipient.

Mrs. Acton continued, "Bill, would you mind opening the portfolio and telling everyone what is inside?"

Bill obliged. He opened it. He apparently didn't see anything inside at first glance. He tilted it toward him, still looking inside. "Two pennies!" he said with excitement.

Now, Mrs. Acton looked surprised. Bill smiled, and so did 34 other class members. Jim broke out laughing, and pretty soon everyone was laughing. Bill let Mrs. Acton know where the pennies came from.

"Bill, is there anything inscribed inside the portfolio?" Mrs. Acton asked.

"Oh, yes, there is!" Bill replied. "Let me see... There's quite a bit...

"I'll read it!" he said excitedly.

The words resonated from Bill loud and clear and firm:

"It says, 'Open your mind'...

' 'Learn' is our foundation word. It is the key to the 'Obstacle Course'. It is the key to life...

'Learn by earnest, thoughtful, action...

'Remember, learning is FUN!...

'You can choose your attitudes...

'One never KNOWS exactly what will happen...

'Think!!! Be creative!!!...

'See beyond the obvious...

'Be prepared to handle challenges by getting proper sleep, nutrition, and exercise...

'Failure can often be good...

'Make every effort work for you...

'Carry your knowledge and experience with you wherever you go."

Bill interrupted his reading to let us know there was just a little more.

He continued:

"'Use your knowledge and experience to teach and help others...

'Fill an empty seat to make it a step stool to a better life.'"

Bill was positively beaming. "Thank you so much!" he told Mrs. Acton.

Clenching the pennies in his hand and clutching the portfolio to his chest, Bill walked over to the chair and sat down.

Suddenly, everyone stood up and gave a thunderous applause.

"We will! We will!" came the cries from the crowd.

"I'm glad I took the course," I thought.

"Thank you, everyone!" Mrs. Acton told us. "I love you all!"

And then it was all over.

"Good Day!" Mrs. Acton said.

We stared in amazement as she abruptly – and quickly – walked out of the room… just like Dr. Acton always had.

Neal R. Voron

"The Obstacle Course"
– Study/Discussion Questions –

- What does Dr. Acton's portfolio represent?

- Is there any significance in the author's repeated references to time when Dr. Acton enters the room for each class? Explain.

- Who is the narrator of the story? Does the viewpoint of the narrator help generate your interest in the story?

- Did you enjoy the story? Why?

- Did you like Dr. Acton? Why?

- Are the names of any of the characters in the story significant? What meanings do they convey?

- Did the story retain your interest throughout? Why or why not? What did the author do that was effective or ineffective in keeping your interest?

- What word does Dr. Acton say is the "foundation word... the key to the "Obstacle Course... the key to life"?

- How does Dr. Acton suggest that his students learn the material he presents in the class?

- Why does Dr. Acton talk about one's "attitude" early in the course? How important does he say is one's attitude towards overcoming obstacles?

- Give an example of the use of semantics in the story. Explain its significance.

- What is an obfuscation? According to Dr. Acton, how does it differ from an obstacle?

- What is the significance of the trip to the Police Development Training Center?

- What is the significance of "Play Day"?

- Do the students in the class "grow" as a result of taking "The Obstacle Course"? Why?/How? Explain.

- What does Dr. Acton's death signify?

- Why did Dr. Acton leave his portfolio to Bill?

- Describe Dr. Acton's teaching style. Would it be effective in the real world? Explain.

- Would the distribution of a course syllabus and a reading list have made Dr. Acton's course more effective or less effective as a teaching tool? Why?

- Did a particular message or example from Dr. Acton really impact your thinking?

- Did "The Obstacle Course" help you view or handle a personal circumstance in a different way? How?

- Would you recommend this book to others? Why?

Feel free to send your comments about
The Obstacle Course to the author, **Neal R. Voron**, at:

nvoron@TheObstacleCourse.com

Neal R. Voron

"The Obstacle Course"
– Dr. Acton's Class Notes –

(1) If you want this course to be helpful to you, open your mind to it.

(2) 'Uncertainty' stops many people from accomplishing things; You did not allow obstacles to block your path, and you are learning here today.

(3) Sometimes we all need to think.

(4) Sometimes we need to ask.

(5) Sometimes we need to ask again.

(6) We must focus our minds to learn that which we are seeking to learn.

(7) We must learn by earnest, thoughtful action.

(8) We must not let interruptions block our course.

(9) Leave your worries at the door; you will do well.

(10) 'Learn' is our foundation word. It is the key to the "Obstacle Course". It is the key to life.

(11) At the core of learning is listening.

(12) For many people, the learning process itself becomes an obstacle.

(13)   Remember, learning is "FUN"!

(14)   Attitude is the way someone acts, feels, or thinks about persons, places, or things.

(15)   People usually view "challenges" as contests that they can win; they perceive "problems" more as insurmountable obstacles.

(16)   You can choose your attitudes towards dealing with situations.

(17)   A person's attitude immensely affects how he or she deals with obstacles. One's attitude itself can become an obstacle.

(18)   One never KNOWS exactly what will happen.

(19)   We only think we know what will happen.

(20)   Our past experiences enable us to make predictions about future events that seem reasonable and dependable, but we cannot be certain predictions will come true.

(21)   We cannot always anticipate the influence of variables.

(22)   We can try to control variables.

(23)   We probably cannot control all variables; we don't know what all of them are.

(24)   We can try to control the variables we are aware of as best as we can.

(25)   We can go forward into the future with an open mind about the influences of unknown variables.

(26)   All sorts of happening possibilities exist regardless of reasonable expectation based upon past habits or experience.

(27)   All sorts of adaptation possibilities exist to handle both expected and unexpected challenges.

(28)   Someone who holds an opportunity for you may be watching to see if you will let obstacles stand in the way of your goals.

*** (29)   Beware: someone who does not want you to reach your goals may put obstacles in your way to try to block you.

(30)   When confronted with an unexpected challenge, be wise enough not to panic, not to jump to conclusions, not to wantonly abandon your goal.

(31)   How you view obstacles and how you respond to them is important.

(32)   Predictions can be helpful, but do not get stuck on them!

(33)   Be flexible and open-minded in your thinking.

(34)   The key is to adapt to whatever occurs in a way that helps you achieve your goals.

(35)   Achieving success by handling challenges you can reasonably expect is easy; It is more difficult to confront unexpected challenges.

(36) You may have to be creative to adapt to a situation.

(37) Sometimes you may adapt in a way that will fail;
But failure can often be good!

(38) Trying and failing may still lead to progress toward a goal.

(39) If you do not try, you will surely fail.

(40) There is a lot to be learned from failure; That knowledge is often worth the price of the effort – it may help you achieve your goals.

(41) Look at dealing with expected & unexpected challenges and confronting potential failure as personal growth opportunities!

(42) Strive for success.

(43) Focus on your goals.

(44) Turn potential negatives into positives.

(45) Make every effort work for you.

(46) One's perspective can affect one's perception of what is correct.

(47) Perspectives and perceptions can differ.

(48) The perspective in which you view things and the perception you form about them are factors which affect your interactions with them.

(49)   You can view things differently and do things differently if you allow yourself to break patterns or to look beyond the familiar.

(50)   Things are not always as they appear.

(51)   Is it that you cannot or will not overcome obstacles?

(52)   Self-imposed limitations are malleable. That means you can change them. They are also expendable. You can get rid of them if you decide to.

(53)   Do you care if you reach your goals?

(54)   Your goals are your goals.

(55)   Only you can destroy your own obstacles.

(56)   You must confront your obstacles if you seek to get past them.

(57)   Others have little power over your personal situation. YOU are the one with the power.

(58)   Viewing obstacles differently could help you destroy them. (View obstacles as obfuscations.)

(59)   Visualization can help you stay focused on your goals and may also help you see another path to reaching them.

(60)   Perceptions and visualizations can help you overcome obstacles.

(61)   It is difficult for some people to visualize their goals clearly without seeing roadblocks.

(62) If you have difficulty with your visualizations, practice them, concentrating on your goal and on eliminating any obstacles that may present themselves.

(63) If your goals are firm in your mind, your mind will seek ways to deal with obstacles.

(64) Obstacles may be helpful.

(65) Obstacles may help you reaffirm – or disaffirm – your commitment to your goals.

(66) Obstacles may present challenges that cause you to pursue educational opportunities or other personal growth experiences.

(67) Obstacles may cause you to seek the help of others who can provide the assistance you need.

(68) Obstacles may help propel you towards your goals, rather than detract you from them.

(69) How you view the challenges you face is extremely important to your ultimate success in achieving your goals.

(70) An obstacle is something that blocks your path, stops you, or pulls you back – anything which stands in the way of your progress.

(71) Obfuscations are things that cloud over, make unclear, or confuse.

(72) Thinking of challenges as obfuscations instead of as obstacles may make the path to one's goals seem more passable.

(73)   YOU choose whether to view challenges as obstacles or as obfuscations.

(74)   YOU choose the path you take toward your goals.

(75)   YOU choose how you are going to respond to the mental images you confront when facing challenges.

(76)   YOU choose whether you are going to let things or people stand in your way.

(77)   The path to your goals may not be as clear as you would like or as easy to travel as you would prefer, but it does not have to be impassable.

(78)   THINK and GROW your way to your goals.

(79)   You carry your lessons with you in your mind.

(80)   Utilization of what you have been taught so that it benefits you makes your acquisition of knowledge worthwhile.

(81)   Unless you deal with your obstacles – or unless they mysteriously disappear on their own – you still carry them with you.

(82)   If you do not have an idea of what your goals are, it is difficult to determine the correct path to attain them.

(83)   To help determine your goals, think about what interests you and think about what you will need to do to achieve whatever those interests are.

(84)   Some people are unwilling or unable to do what is necessary to achieve their goals.

(85)   Prioritizing your interests can help you determine where to direct your efforts to achieve your goals.

(86)   Remember, priorities can change.

(87)   Consider wants versus needs. Which takes priority for you?

(88)   Are your challenges self-imposed? Perhaps you can unimpose them.

(89)   Play manifests healthful, restorative, creative energy.

(90)   Play can help you to feel better, to express your creativity, to communicate, to learn, to understand, to see possibilities, and to grow into the person you wish to be.

(91)   You can make "Play Day" any day and every day.

(92)   We can see beyond the obvious if we seek to.

(93)   The real world we live in is constantly changing. Too often we become stuck both in our thinking and in how we approach change.

(94)   Each situation is unique and must be addressed based upon its unique circumstances. What worked before may not work again.

(95)   By going forth with a plan, we face challenges proactively.

(96)   Without a plan, or by adjusting a plan when necessary, we face challenges reactively.

(97)   It is important to be appropriately proactive and reactive to achieve the greatest success.

(98)   Prepare to handle any challenges you may face: get proper sleep, nutrition, and exercise.

(99)   If you are not feeling fit and well, it is difficult to perform optimally.

(100) What you feed your mind is as important as what you feed your body.

~ ~ ~ ~ ~

Webmasters, Employers, Schools, Organizations...

Share *Dr. Acton's Class Notes* with your audiences! For details:

http://www.TheObstacleCourse.com/share.htm

Neal R. Voron

"The Obstacle Course"
– Reader Comments –

We hope you enjoyed reading *The Obstacle Course* by **Neal R. Voron**. Any comments you would wish to share with the author would be greatly appreciated.

Please submit your comments by sending your answers to the following questions in an e-mail directly to Neal at nvoron@TheObstacleCourse.com . Thank you.

Name:

Email Address:

Company or Organization:

Your Street Address:

City:

State:

Postal Code:

Country:

Phone Number (Include Area Code):

Your Occupation:

- Please share your comments about **The Obstacle Course** by Neal R. Voron:

- Would you like to be informed via e-mail when additional writings by Neal R. Voron are available for review?

- Do you give your permission for Neal R. Voron to freely use your comments above (with your name, occupation, and organization affiliation) for publicity purposes without compensation?

If you have any private (not-to-be published) comments about **The Obstacle Course** that you wish to share with the author, Neal R. Voron, kindly include them below:

About The Author...
Neal R. Voron

Neal R. Voron, author of ***The Obstacle Course***, is a writer, lyricist, and entrepreneur who believes in the power of communications to "make a difference" in people's lives and in society as a whole.

Neal is the president of **Voron Communications**, Philadelphia, PA, and the co-founder, with Joseph F.M. Pokorny, of **RyKy Records (tm)**. His writings, song lyrics, and creative Internet communications ventures are all part of Voron's efforts to share the benefits of his personal experiences and creative insights with a global audience.

It was Neal's interest in getting ***The Obstacle Course*** published that led to his involvement with the Internet and, subsequently, to his other endeavors.

Over the years, Voron pioneered the development of some web sites that served then-underserved audiences. His former "Night Shift Initiative" web site helped to educate and benefit thousands of shiftworkers, their families, and their employers about coping with the shiftwork lifestyle. His early web site about email autoresponders similarly introduced many individuals and businesses to the responsible use of a valuable Internet communications tool.

Neal's online publication of the lyrics to **We Thought She'd Live Forever**, a song he co-wrote with Joseph F.M. Pokorny years before, ultimately led to the launch of RyKy Records after a visitor to his little-publicized web site asked about the availability of the song on CD.

Voron and Pokorny, acquaintances for 15 years, got back in touch with each other, and Voron – amazed at Pokorny's treasure vault of then-over 700 unreleased original songs – decided to launch and build RyKy Records into a truly special music label that would endeavor to touch people's hearts and souls.

With RyKy Records, he and Joseph F.M. Pokorny truly are "Making A Difference With Music (tm)", having already released many inspirational and emotionally touching songs – like **Maybe Tomorrow, For Your Dreams, Dream The American Dream, We The People, For The Heroes,** and others – and **Wind Dance,** an Irish love story, the first of many musicals and cantatas planned.

We Thought She'd Live Forever was one of the songs released on RyKy's first album, and it ultimately became a climactic song in Pokorny's **Wind Dance Musical**. After reading Voron's self-help/inspirational novel, **The Obstacle Course**, Pokorny became inspired to create **The Obstacle Course Musical**.

Since RyKy's launch, Voron has co-written several more songs with Pokorny: **Starting Over, Please Do Not Call Me, Please Do Not Spam Me,** and **Can The Spam,** and he has inspired the creation of many other songs.

Besides **The Obstacle Course,** Neal has written **The Spider's Dream Web,** a mythical story for children and web lovers everywhere about the birth of the Internet's World Wide Web, and **The Musician's Christmas Dream,** a Christmas story about a musician's dream to share his music with the world.

Neal is also the founder of the **Motivation Inspiration Month** and **Resolution Kick-Off Day** celebrations held in January, and is the developer of **AffiliateMarketingPower.com**, **LyricSongbooks.com**, and other web sites.

Voron earned a bachelor of arts degree in Journalism and Communications in 1983 from Point Park University. He is a 1979 graduate of Central High School, Philadelphia, PA (238th class).

Neal and his wife, Barbarann, a psychotherapist in private practice, reside in Philadelphia with their two children, Ryan and Kyle.

Neal R. Voron

Enjoy The Story?
You've GOT To Hear The Musical...

'The Obstacle Course Musical'!
Written and Composed by
Joseph Francis Michael Pokorny

Neal R. Voron, author of *The Obstacle Course*, is pleased to inform fans of Dr. Acton that the story inspired a musical CD album created by America's truly remarkable songwriter, **Joseph Francis Michael Pokorny**!

"The Obstacle Course Musical" brings *The Obstacle Course* into new dimensions of creativity, enlightenment, and entertainment! Its sound and rhythm move Dr. Acton and his students from the classroom to the big stage!

The Obstacle Course Musical's song line-up includes:

1. The Obstacle Course
2. Step By Step
3. Close The Door
4. Number Twenty-Nine Beware
5. Starting Over
6. And I Love You
7. Survival
8. Can You Tell Me Why?
9. For The Heroes
10. A Change Of Heart
11. Starlight
12. With Your Heart And With Your Soul

13. Gone
14. Maybe
15. Learn
16. The Obstacle Course (Reprise)

Learn more at:

http://www.TheObstacleCourseMusical.com

For more music from **Joseph Francis Michael Pokorny**, visit:

http://www.RyKyRecords.com

Dear Reader,

Someone cared enough about you to put this book in your hands. Perhaps that person was a friend, a relative, a teacher, or a colleague. Or, perhaps that person was YOU, yourself.

Whoever that person was, I believe, gave you a special gift… not just a tale about an old man and his class of students, but an affirmation of their own belief and confidence in YOUR potential to be successful in the "obstacle course" of life.

That is because *The Obstacle Course* serves not only as an entertaining story, but also as a catalyst to open your mind to a wider world of means and possibilities to accomplish whatever you seek to achieve in life.

What you ultimately gain from your reading of this story, though, is up to YOU and how you decide to embrace the attitudes and ideas it presents. I hope you find the adventures of Dr. Acton to be both enjoyable and helpful.

If you feel that having read *The Obstacle Course* has benefited you, consider "making a difference" in other people's lives by letting them know about the story and/or handing them "gifts" of their own copies of this book.

I invite you to join the **Dr. Acton Fan Club** and to sign-up for the periodic **Dr. Acton Fan Club newsletter** online at http:// www.TheObstacleCourse.com. The web site also provides special resources, links and offers for Fan Club members.

Your interest in *The Obstacle Course* is sincerely appreciated. Feel free to send me comments at: nvoron@TheObstacleCourse. com

Sincerely,
Neal R. Voron

CPSIA information can be obtained at www.ICGtesting.com
Printed in the USA
BVOW03s1848210514

354217BV00001B/73/A

9 781418 447397